'Gutsy, gritty and good, Dame Susan's forthright commentary on her remarkable life is delivered with dollops of warmth and lashings of humour. A rollicking story of a life well lived.' PETRA BAGUST

'You can hear Susan's voice as you read it . . . She is, as always, blunt, honest, wise and warm. And funny — the throwaway story about the spear-gun is worth the price of admission alone.' MICHÈLE A'COURT

'This is a story about digging deep. About learning. About wanting to be better. I've met few people who've reinvented themselves so determinedly. From squash player to Race Relations Commissioner. From working class kid to a Dame. This is the story of becoming Suzy D — in all her determined, triumphant and unabashed singularity.' JOHN CAMPBELL

Dame Suzy D
My Story

SUSAN DEVOY

Dame Suzy D
My Story

ALLEN&UNWIN
AUCKLAND·SYDNEY·MELBOURNE·LONDON

First published in 2024

Copyright © Susan Devoy 2024

Allen & Unwin
Level 2, 10 College Hill, Freemans Bay
Auckland 1011, New Zealand
+64 (9) 377 3800
auckland@allenandunwin.com
www.allenandunwin.co.nz

83 Alexander Street
Crows Nest NSW 2065, Australia
+61 (2) 8425 0100

A catalogue record for this book is available from the
National Library of New Zealand.

ISBN 978 1 99100 652 3

Design by Kate Barraclough
Set in Tiempos Text and ITC Avant Garde Gothic
Cover photograph by Matt Klitscher
Printed and bound in Australia by the Opus Group

10 9 8 7 6 5 4 3 2 1

MIX
Paper | Supporting
responsible forestry
FSC
www.fsc.org   FSC® C001695

To the main men in my life:
John, Julian, Alex, Josh and Jamie

Contents

One
The Bonds
of Family

I ALWAYS CRINGED when people would say, 'Gosh you are so much like your mother Tui.'

Don't get me wrong — I loved my mother to bits, but I found some things about her annoying and embarrassing. I know my sons probably — well, not probably, they *do* — feel the same way about me. First up, Mum had no filter, so whatever came into her head came out her mouth. This often meant that if your opinion differed from hers, you could expect a tongue lashing.

Mum loved ringing talkback radio shows. I would be driving home late at night from a tournament or exhibition series and I would hear her dulcet tones on the airwaves. She had her favourite hosts and, given that they all knew she was my mother, my name would be the first thing that came up in conversation.

It drove me nuts! I tried asking her to stop — I even asked if she would mind using a pseudonym. So rather than Tui from Rotorua she became Mavis from Hastings, but that didn't fool anyone.

She thought she was a sporting encyclopaedia — and to her credit she was an avid follower of sport — and would happily offer her analysis of every rugby and cricket match played. When the Warriors were established she became their biggest fan, probably because she was the most vocal supporter of the Mad Butcher.

Back in the day, squash clubs held infamous Saturday-night parties. I was always embarrassed watching her front and centre on the dance floor, but man, she had some moves. If she wasn't dancing, she was holding court at the bar; she and my father were often the last to leave the building.

All these years later I admire those traits, and I'm happy to admit I am a chip off the old block in more ways than one. I don't ring talkback and am not a smooth mover, but I do like a good party and I'm not ashamed to say I have been known to let my hair down. I hardly touched alcohol during my sporting days, but I've spent the past 30 years catching up. I don't have much of a filter either and I'm not afraid to say what's on my mind, even if it makes me unpopular.

I now regret admonishing my mother rather than applauding her for a life of hard work and sacrifice. The women of my mother's generation were hard doers. It has taken four children of my own for me to recognise that.

TUI AND JOHN WERE ECSTATIC when I was born at Rotorua Hospital on 4 January 1964. Dad, as was the custom in those days, did not attend my birth. Dr Sill, our family doctor, rang him with the good news that after six sons he finally had a new model. He bought a new Vauxhall to celebrate. But despite having a new car, my brothers said we never went anywhere because there were too many of us.

Naming me was quite a drama apparently. My six brothers all felt they had a say in this important decision, so a sweepstake was held and my name drawn out of a hat. I have never been told what the other options were. So Susan it was, with middle names Elizabeth and Anne to placate the grandmothers.

My eldest brother was sixteen when I was born, and the youngest was five. Our house and our lives were best described as rambunctious. Nine of us lived in a three-bedroom state house in Puriri Crescent, Rotorua. The boys' room was akin to a school dormitory with five tiny single beds, each with a little night-light and cubby-hole. I slept in Mum and Dad's room. My mother would joke that I was the only contraceptive that worked. Given that they were Catholics and any form of contraception was forbidden, Mum was grateful she only had seven children. She used to joke — but I knew she was deadly serious — that she was lucky she didn't have fourteen. The third bedroom was reserved for me when I was older, and for whichever brother needed the most peace and quiet in the meantime. I have never been able to fathom how that was determined.

My mother worked hard — there really wasn't any alternative. She used to say, 'Hard work never killed anyone.' She was right in her case, but a full-time job on top of running a busy household didn't leave time for much else, including herself.

When I was six weeks old Mum went back to work and I was bundled off each morning to Mrs Harris down the road. I don't remember that, but I do remember later going to Poppies Daycare in Marguerita Street, and sitting in the large bay window at the end of every day waiting for Mum to pick me up.

Mum worked in my dad's accountancy practice. She wasn't a qualified accountant but she ran the show, just like she did at home. At the time I totally failed to appreciate the disproportionate workload women shouldered, especially if they were working mums. We moaned because none of us were allowed to buy jeans — Mum drew the line at having to wash them, which I quite understand now, given that she had an old wringer washing machine and nobody had clothes dryers back then.

She cooked and fed an army and was a dab hand with the sewing machine. Apparently I point-blank refused to wear the beautiful smocked dresses she made me. My older brothers were at boarding school in Wellington and when she made the long trip there to visit them she would stock up on bolts of lovely fabric and painstakingly sew these dresses, smocking and tatting amazing designs. She loved fashion and always looked immaculate herself, so I must have been a major disappointment in that department, especially as the only daughter. I obstinately refused from a young age to wear any dresses, so Mum gave them to a friend who proudly gave them to her granddaughter.

When that friend of Mum's died, years after my mother, I attended her funeral. After the service I introduced myself to the woman who gave the eulogy and discovered that she was the recipient of those magnificent dresses. Katherine has much more fashion sense than I do so Mum would have been delighted to find someone who appreciated her beautiful work.

Nothing much has changed — I still detest wearing dresses and avoid them at all costs. My eldest son is getting married soon and my social media is already full of suggested mother-of-the-groom dresses. I am dreading the thought. Shame I can't wear my trackpants.

There wasn't anything my mother couldn't or didn't do. She painted and wallpapered, cooked, cleaned, sewed, gardened — and worked full time. She was a powerhouse, and we all took it for granted.

We learnt early on not to cross her. Our mother took no prisoners.

From the age of five I would walk 2 kilometres to and from St Mary's primary school each day. My brother was supposed to accompany me but the novelty of having to mind his baby sister quickly wore off. I was a wee dot and I recall being accosted on more than one occasion by one particular college student. He would wait for me at the end of a thoroughfare I took as a shortcut home. He would get off his bike and start masturbating in front of me.

I didn't comprehend what he was doing and was more confused than frightened. I told my parents about one encounter. Weirdly, it wasn't my father who took matters into his own hands, it was my pint-sized mother. She was ropable. She lay in wait one day and ambushed the guy. He got a tongue lashing and a bloody good hiding with her umbrella.

Suffice to say it never happened again. That was a funny day because I had also told my mother about the creepy old pervert who sat on a swing in the park wearing no underwear, so Mum sorted him out too. He didn't quite suffer the same fate with the umbrella but was scared enough that I never saw him again either. Mum was a formidable force and never shied away from confrontation.

WE WERE A SPORTS-MAD FAMILY. Like many typical Kiwi boys my brothers played a lot of sport growing up — rugby, cricket, football and tennis. There was great interest when the Brownlees, a well-known squash family, opened the first squash club in Rotorua. My brothers went along to try it out and were hooked; even Mum and Dad played, albeit on a casual basis. The social side and the family environment were as attractive as the game itself, and that's what drew our family in. Needless to say the Devoy family name soon became synonymous with squash in Rotorua.

In the early 1970s we made regular trips to tournaments all over New Zealand, and often to Auckland. Squashed (excuse the pun) into the Vauxhall, our first stop was always the Te Rapa Tavern. Gerard, Julian and I would be left in the car with a bag of chips and a Coke while Mum and Dad nipped in for a couple of quick jugs. Then we would weave our way to Auckland.

I was too young to play, but after the games were finished for the day and everyone was in the bar, I would borrow one of my brothers' rackets and simply hit the ball for hours — generally until the last pint was pulled. I would even sneak on between matches or any moment a court came free.

Thank God back then pubs were closed on Sundays when we made the return trip. Instead it was a pie and a doughnut from Shands Bakery in Huntly. Often my fellow passengers were a little the worse for wear and the trips home were a bit subdued. Sometimes we would have to endure a lengthy post-mortem.

Mum and Dad were not overzealous parents living their lives vicariously through their offspring but there was, I sensed, a feeling of frustration that my talented brothers showed a distinct preference for the social side of the game rather than putting in the hard yards training. This, my parents felt, stopped them from reaching their full potential. It was an early life lesson for me: that talent will only take you so far.

My childhood circumstances played a massive role in making me the resilient and independent person I am. While I was doted on as the youngest, Mum and Dad were so busy keeping their heads above water that we were often left to our own devices. The squash club — first T Street and then Geyser City — became my second home; if I was ever unaccounted for, everyone knew where I would be. There was always someone I knew at the club. I would badger anyone who came near the place to hit with me, and when those options were exhausted I was happy to practise on my own. The legendary Colin Brownlee took me under his wing and if he wasn't offering me coaching advice, we were plotting which tournament we were going to enter and what adventure we would go on next.

I remember so many great families — the Munros, the Te Kanis, the McQueens, the Smiths, the Wyatts — most in one way or another still involved with squash.

OUR HOME AT 19 PURIRI CRESCENT was affectionately known as Tui's Diner. One of the rooms of our three-bedroom house had been extended to accommodate the growing family. We had a large section that was home to some monumental backyard clashes.

Tui and John were social butterflies. They loved company, a beer or three, and were often the first on the dance floor. At the end of a big night out, regardless of the hour, everyone knew Mum would happily produce steak, eggs and chips for all-comers, washed down with another cold beer, and join in the partying until the early hours. Dad was equally social; they both loved nothing more than a houseful of visitors.

So you might say partying is in our blood! My brothers are all great dancers, having had weekly lessons at Irene Oliver's school of dance. I am still puzzled as to why my mother thought dancing was essential for the men in our family while I was sent off instead to speech lessons with Olga Archer. I can't dance to save myself, but thankfully I can string a few words together.

John Oakley, now my husband, was the first boy I took home to meet my parents. My parents were both heavy smokers and he recalls walking through the kitchen into the dining room through a low cloud of smoke and haze. There were my parents at midday with the big DB bottles of beer. 'Have a drink, son,' they said, and John thought, well, a bit early in the day, but it would be rude not to. He soon realised what a character my mother was. He'd only just met her and she said, 'Right, we're off to Smallbone Park. Northern Districts are playing Canterbury [John's team],' and off they went for an afternoon's cricket.

Large families have large gatherings, and they are my

fondest memories. I relished any time we could all be together. We were never big on gifts; it was more important for everyone to be present. Christmas was a big deal — brothers, wives and girlfriends, aunties, uncles and cousins would arrive en masse. Then there were family weddings and of course the arrival of nieces and nephews. I was only eleven when I first became an aunty and thought it was Christmas to have all these new members of our large brood.

Birthdays were a non-event. There were no presents or big celebrations except on the milestone birthdays. My mother as she got older would ring me on the third of January to wish me a happy birthday, if she remembered, and I would say, 'It's tomorrow but today is your wedding anniversary.' She had forgotten that too.

Of course it wasn't always happy families.

Fun family occasions could quickly turn sour, and the common denominator was always alcohol. One minute every-thing seemed hunky dory and then suddenly someone would say the wrong thing and *BOOM*. Tempers would flare and it would all turn to custard. It seldom got physical — the culprits were generally too inebriated — but it certainly ruined the occasion. I hated it, particularly when I was younger. I was always trying to keep the peace.

The next day, despite people being a little sheepish, things would be back to normal. Either no one could remember what happened or they would pretend it hadn't. We didn't sit around like mature adults and thrash it out. I'm not sure if it was driven by the excess of male energy or if it was just a Devoy thing, but we all found it difficult to discuss any issues we had with each other until a skinful gave us the necessary Dutch courage.

Age has mellowed us and we look back now with an acknowledgement that this behaviour was not something we're proud of. We laugh and cringe about it now.

I would best describe us siblings as being like the Mafia in the sense that loyalty runs deep — any one of us would be there in a flash if another needed help. We may not have always seen eye to eye, but cross one of us and you take on the whole mob. We all love and value family, our family, despite all our imperfections.

I WAS 29 AND A new mum when my father passed away in 1993. In many ways it was a relief for all of us. A year earlier he had suffered a major stroke and then got liver cancer. I remember my last conversation with him, although it wasn't really a conversation because he couldn't communicate properly. It was heart-breaking. He knew he was dying: strangely, nothing was said but everything was understood. I had to go back to Auckland and told him I would see him the next day. I did — but at the funeral home.

My mother had cared for him since his stroke and it had been tough, so I was relieved for her. She was only 67 so had a lot of living left to do. But she never recovered from losing her soulmate, and she became bitter. She blamed everyone — especially God, and never set foot inside a church again. I got the feeling it was a one-finger salute.

What God would do this?

I had retired from professional squash the year before, and didn't realise at the time how much of a void this created in her life. Sure, that had been replaced by new grandchildren, but she already had plenty of those and didn't hide the fact that she had done her time looking after children. The novelty had well and truly worn off.

My playing career and my success had been a large part of her life. She would say, 'I can't walk downtown — too many people want to stop and talk about you!' She loved it of course. Whenever I visited she asked me to take her to the supermarket. Not to buy groceries but on the off chance that she would see someone she knew or who knew me, and they would want to stop and chat.

My mother was 38 when I was born, and I was 37 when she died in 2001. Since then I have grown to love all the things about her that once irked me, and at times have been wracked with guilt. She knew I loved her but I am not sure I showed enough gratitude for all the sacrifices she made over her life for all of us.

It was tough for us as she aged, which seemed to accelerate after our father died. She stopped taking care of herself so she moved into a rest home. I toyed with the idea of bringing her to live with us in Auckland but I knew she wouldn't want to leave Rotorua, where she had lived most of her life. In some ways that was a relief, as I'm not sure how any of us would have coped with four young boys and my mother in the same house.

I got down to see her as often as I could. I'd pile my boys in the car and we would get to the rest home to be greeted by the same four women sitting in the foyer. They all had dementia so the conversation was always the same. 'Hello, you have four boys, what are their names?' Then we would bustle off to see Nana.

Rest homes are not equipped for young boisterous children so it was always a short visit, then Mum would say, 'Well, okay, you can go now.' On our way out we would meet the same four ladies and the conversation would be repeated. Some of the boys remember that.

No sooner would we get back to my brother's house in Rotorua, where we stayed, than my phone would ring and Mum would ask when we were visiting again. To my shame, I found it tiresome and frustrating. She was my mother and I was her only daughter, but it wasn't the relationship I had expected as she got older. What I wouldn't give now to have that time again — or even that phone call.

I don't have a sister or a daughter so there is this void of not having that one woman in your life you can share anything with.

I was with my mother when she died. Despite her newfound antipathy towards the church, I asked the priest, a family friend, to come and give her the last rites. She was still an avid Warriors fan and after administering the last rites Father Timmerman told her she could go now, firstly because the Warriors' losing streak had been broken, but more importantly because God and my dad were waiting for her. Mum never regained conscious-ness but the tears slid down her face. Perhaps she had simply been waiting for the all-clear.

IT SEEMS THE DEVOY CLAN are not destined to make old bones. Losing your parents is tough, but losing a sibling is a lot more confronting. It's like the chain is broken and you start questioning your own mortality.

Brendan, my eldest brother, died when he was 65 — too young and so unfair. He was the self-appointed leader of our family and I was always his baby sister, never mind that I had children of my own. I remember one day telling him, 'It's okay — I'm not thirteen anymore.'

He died in 2013 after a battle with melanoma. It was a bit like my dad — Brendan was an honest toiler all his life and suddenly, on the verge of retirement, his supposed golden years were gone, just like that.

Local hospice staff were angels and he was at home until he died, with his family around him. The sound of his grandchildren carrying on oblivious to what was happening was the relief everyone needed. My other brothers struggled, all sitting on the deck with a beer, no one knowing what to say. Brendan was barely conscious at the end and saying goodbye was heart-wrenching for all of us.

Just a couple of years later I was at a function in Hamilton with my race relations commissioner hat on and a woman came up and asked about my brother Michael. Michael was a year younger than Brendan and had recently retired from teaching after nearly 40 years at Fairfield Intermediate. He was still doing some relief teaching.

Michael had always been a creature of habit and was a stalwart of his local pub in Hamilton. He went there every day to catch up with his mates, put a bet on a racehorse. For years he had run the weekly quiz night and was quite the local identity. So when she said they hadn't seen Michael at the pub for a couple of weeks, alarm bells started ringing.

I had to go on to Auckland for work, but my gut instinct made me detour back to Hamilton that night on the way home to Tauranga. It wasn't late and Michael's wife was out babysitting their grandkids. It took an age for him to get to the door. He looked ghastly and I was taken aback. He explained that he was exhausted and it was clear he had lost a lot of weight. He was patiently waiting for a referral from the doctor to see someone at the hospital.

I was heading off to Melbourne for Labour weekend but I rang my other brothers to alert them. I had no idea what was wrong with Michael but told them he didn't look great.

John and I were walking some of the Great Ocean Walk, where we had intermittent cellphone coverage, but I got a text to say Michael had had a massive stroke and was in Waikato Hospital. I made a mad dash back to Melbourne to get on the first plane home. I will always be grateful for making it before he passed away.

There are always tender moments that lighten tragic times. When the undertaker arrived after Brendan's death, he was asked if he could toot as he drove away with the coffin in the hearse because Brendan would always toot for his grandkids when he was leaving. He duly did, and young Max piped up: 'That's not Poppa, he's in the boot.'

It was similar with Michael, who was barely conscious when I got there. His son Liam was expecting their first baby and asked everyone to leave the room so he could confidentially tell Michael the sex of the baby. My son Alex was with me, and Liam invited him to stay. Alex, knowing his mother only too well, said, 'No, Mum will have that information out of me before we get home.'

We joked none of us were making old bones and then my third brother, Paul, who was fast approaching 70, was diagnosed with throat cancer. Suddenly it wasn't so funny anymore. The treatment for throat cancer is about as brutal as it gets but Paul was stoic. I suppose thinking about the alternative keeps you going. Thankfully he made it through, but it was tough.

Julian, my fifth brother, has had a melanoma scare. I try not to think about it but it does prey at the back of one's mind. How could it not?

I hope I make old bones; I hope I get to be a grandmother.

Two
My Squash
Career

I RETIRED FROM professional squash on 10 October 1992.

That finals day was different from the previous three World Champs.

It felt like the first day of the rest of my life.

Normally on finals day I would be consumed with the fear of losing; instead I was uncharacteristically calm. I knew that, win or lose, I was hanging up my racket for good. John and I had often talked about it and I could hear him thinking, *Here we go again — she won't go through with it.*

Each World Champs final and British Open he would buy a new tie. It was a ritual — he always wore a suit and bought a new tie. The tie would have some significance to where we were, or to the event. That day's new tie was emblazoned with Mickey

Mouse dressed up as a mounted policeman, because we were in Canada.

As I was ironing it, I looked up and said, 'Today's the day.'

For the past couple of years I had found it a real struggle to find joy in doing what I loved most. For years I had thrived on training and competing and winning. Squash was my passion, but passion is not just about loving something — it is about sacrificing everything to achieve your goals. And I couldn't do it anymore.

It had been a stellar year. All going well, I was about to go out on top, as the current Swedish, Irish, New Zealand, Australian, French, Hong Kong, Scottish and British Open champion. I was going out on my own terms.

But the demons of the year before still haunted me.

THAT YEAR, 1991, HAD BEEN my *annus horribilis*. It had started with a lot of change that I didn't like one bit. The Buckingham-shire club where I had been based for the past six years had undergone major changes — squash was no longer their priority so there was no one left to train with.

John, my trusty husband and sidekick, training partner, manager and confidant, was back in New Zealand establishing a career while I travelled. We both knew the squash dream was not going to last forever and it had not made me a millionaire.

I was reminded how lonely touring can be.

Our home away from home for almost a decade had been a flat in a beautiful English village called Marlow in the county of Buckinghamshire, situated on the Thames River. It was a short trip to London and close to Heathrow. It was idyllic.

John arrived just in time for the British Open, his usual upbeat optimistic self. It had been the longest time we had spent apart, and he, like so many others, probably took it for granted I was going to win again. As far as he was concerned, I was on track to take my eighth consecutive British Open.

He had missed being on the circuit with me — let's face it, it's a cool life jet-setting around Europe while your partner does all the work! I say that tongue in cheek — I had missed him dreadfully. I had become so accustomed to having my team around me I just wasn't used to doing it all on my own. But everyone — including me — knows that I am made of tough stuff, and nothing takes precedence over training, irrespective of what's going on around me, so I had put in the work.

Each time I won the British Open I would think nothing could be this hard, but every year defending my title got a little bit harder. I had set the standard and I had to keep beating it. For me the British Open was the Holy Grail of squash. It was the doorway to my becoming the best in the world so it was special each and every time.

That year the lead-up to the quarter-finals went well and nothing suggested I was not on track to win. I loved the atmosphere at Wembley Stadium where the all-glass court was set up.

Then the unthinkable happened: I lost in the quarter-final to a very spirited English player, Sue Wright. For me this was nothing short of catastrophic and I could sense the ripples spreading through the stadium.

The press conference afterwards felt like a firing squad.

Journalists peppered me with questions and I always take it so personally, as if they are enjoying the torture when they have me in their sights. I told them what they wanted to hear because it was true: Sue Wright was too good today.

Sportsmanship is important and I prided myself on being professional on and off the court. I was gracious in defeat, bit my lip and made sure there were no tears, but I could not wait to get out of the place.

My support crew knew to stay clear and let me stew for a few days. John took off on a holiday that had become an annual event — he always went golfing with a group of friends after the British Open. That suited me fine — I wanted to be on my own, with space to reflect. To pour salt on my wounds, telegrams started arriving from back home wishing me luck in the final.

When it was time to return to New Zealand I didn't really want to go. For seven consecutive years my homecoming had meant a flood of congratulations and media hype, but this time would be very different. The people who mattered didn't care, but I couldn't get my head around it. I was embarrassed to be going home a loser.

Still smarting from ruining my record, I got back into training and playing the local circuit, and pretty soon all seemed right with the world once more. Perhaps losing had made me more human — or made others appreciate how hard I worked to stay at the top. The only pressure was the pressure I put on myself.

I was getting ready to head off to play in Australia but I felt a bit off — a tad lethargic and out of sorts. We had no Dr Google back in those days and I don't know why but I had an inkling and bought a home pregnancy test kit.

When John came home from work that night I said, 'I've got something to tell you. You won't believe it, but I'm pregnant.'

Shock and amazement were plastered all over his face. I hadn't had a period for years so we had assumed I wasn't even ovulating. We couldn't believe it. Suddenly I didn't have to worry about the future of my squash career: the decision was made for me. This was simply meant to be.

Once we got over the initial excitement we had some decisions to make. I was due to fly to Australia in a couple of days to play in the South Australian and Australian Opens. I had no idea whether it was safe for me to play or not. We consulted my doctor and decided that as I had been playing and training without any problems, I would probably be fine to carry on. Everything was arranged and it seemed logical to see it through, especially as this was probably going to be my last trip.

I felt half-hearted about these tournaments by then, but we didn't tell anyone I was pregnant at this stage so I had to pretend everything was normal.

I won the 1991 South Australian Open, beating Liz Irving in the final. Liz was one of the nicest girls on the circuit and although I tried hard to keep the news to myself, I couldn't contain myself and ended up telling her. Suddenly it seemed very real.

As I arrived in Melbourne for the Australian Open I began to feel nauseous, with a few stomach pains. I was apprehensive — was this normal? I didn't know whether I was doing the right thing playing and didn't know who to ask.

I carried on but my heart wasn't in it. I barely tried in the semis, which was not like me, and when I lost that got people talking. Off the court officials and players were muttering among themselves, wondering what was wrong with me.

I avoided the press and took the first flight home. The media in New Zealand had a sniff something was up so we decided to front-foot it and contacted Bob Pearce, an old mate from the *New Zealand Herald*, and he broke the story. My pregnancy was front-page news and everyone was delighted.

I felt obliged to carry on and play in the New Zealand Open. I spoke to various women who had played competitive sport early in their pregnancies and all insisted I would be fine. The only trouble was that I didn't feel right.

I travelled to Hamilton for the tournament and my sister-in-law organised for me to have a scan and see a specialist. Walking into that doctor's room I sensed there might be something wrong. The specialist gently explained there were problems, and there was a 50/50 chance I would lose this baby. I was bereft and consumed by guilt. I thought that continuing to play had put me in this position — it was no one's fault but my own.

My mind was made up. I was on my way to tell the tournament organisers I was withdrawing when my sister-in-law rushed up and said, 'Don't panic but your father has taken a turn behind the wheel of his car.' They had been driving over to watch me play. She said he was okay but had been taken to Waikato Hospital.

We rushed there immediately. Seeing the nurses and doctors all around him, I realised it was serious. Mum didn't seem to be aware of the enormity of the situation.

Dad had had a stroke. When we went in he looked a bit shaken but was alert and sitting up. They assured us they were doing everything they could. Eventually we all went home to my brother Mark's place.

I woke up in the middle of the night in excruciating pain. John rang the specialist I had seen earlier in the day and he met us at the hospital. He told me I was miscarrying and soon I would be in theatre, and it would all be over. Within 24 hours I had learnt there was an issue with my pregnancy, my father had had a stroke, and I lost my baby.

If I thought things couldn't get any worse, I was wrong. During the night my father suffered a second, major stroke. We were told he might never recover, and certainly would never be the same.

We were all devastated.

The next few weeks were a blur. Dad stayed in Waikato Hospital for a long time, unable to walk or talk. His inability to communicate with us broke my heart — he looked at us intently and tried so hard.

Mum's life had suddenly been turned upside down and it all seemed so unfair, so unjust. Dad had retired at 70, after a lifetime in which they had both worked their butts off. Finally they'd had the chance to kick back and put their feet up, and now this. What was their future? Would my father survive this? Would he talk and walk again? Losing a baby at that time just seemed — I don't know, less of a big deal. I could have another baby. I couldn't get another father. At that point I felt I had over-invested in squash when what was important was my family.

Sadly, it had taken something catastrophic to put things into perspective.

Eventually Dad was transferred to Rotorua Hospital. I felt no desire to pick up a racket and was spending most of my time at the hospital helping Mum, who was struggling to cope and be Dad's cheerleader. When someone cannot talk, you just keep talking yourself, to fill in the long awkward pauses.

The physiotherapy was relentless and I saw the pain and frustration etched on my dad's face. But there was gradual improvement and eventually he got to go home. It was not the recovery we all wanted but he could shuffle along with a stick. He spent most of his time sitting in a chair watching television, sipping an occasional beer through a straw.

I struggled to process everything. I didn't know how to deal with the grief of losing a baby, and Dad's poor health was a distraction. It quickly became like the miscarriage had never happened. I just knew my father and mother needed me, and I needed them. Life was never going to be the same for any of us.

I was avoiding any decisions about my own future when my hand was forced. My number one world ranking was dependent on my entering and winning a certain number of tournaments each year. Because of the miscarriage I had had poor results in Australia and Britain in 1991, and had withdrawn from the New Zealand and Singapore Opens.

I had applied to WISPA, the international professional organisation, to have my Singapore result waived on compassionate grounds. However, they insisted that a miscarriage was like any other injury and I would be awarded zero points. So for the first time in eight years I looked set to lose my top ranking. I *had* to play and win the upcoming Dutch Open.

My parents' reaction clinched the deal. They were relieved when I said I was going. I had forgotten the joy and pleasure they got from following my career. We all needed a sense of purpose, and I knew then that this could be good for all of us.

I jumped on a plane, travelled 24 hours and more, won the tournament and flew back just in time for Christmas. My feet barely touched the ground but I dug deep. My greatest strength is the ability to perform when the stakes are highest.

I had got my mojo back; now I knew I had unfinished business.

THIRTY YEARS ON, I AM mortified to look back and realise my obsession with winning. The mantra 'winning is not everything, it is the *only* thing' dominated my psyche. I could not accept defeat as anything but complete failure.

In my era we didn't have 'sport science'. Everyone was a little sceptical about sports psychologists — in fact we would joke that if you had to see one of those then you were *really* screwed up. Nobody placed much emphasis on the mental side — with sport, you either had it or you didn't.

Ironically, I was mentally stronger than many of my competitors on the court, but off the court the nerves and pressure took a toll that I hid from the world — and even from John to a certain extent. Except when I became a raving lunatic and there was no escaping it. I would bottle everything up for a while and then he would cop it.

Talking to the right person might have made a difference but I didn't talk about or openly admit to any failings, because to do so would have demonstrated weakness. Fear of failure dogged my sporting life. I would have made a great case study.

All the experts say that fear is a debilitating factor, yet for me the fear of losing was my strongest motivation. The first British Open, the first World Championship, winning at home in New Zealand in 1987 were all euphoric moments, occasions I relished and celebrated. The other triumphs brought relief because when you have been at the top for so long everyone expects you to stay there — and more importantly so did I!

With the benefit of age and wisdom, I now realise that up till then my entire life had focused on *one thing*. I had done nothing else. I had got to the top at a young age and stayed there, and I didn't know anything different. My normal wasn't normal at all.

I was the best in the world for nearly ten years because I trained the hardest of anyone on the circuit. While my skills and technique training were as sophisticated as they could be, my fitness training could best be described as maniacal.

Inevitably before a major event I would get sick, which was my body's way of telling me I needed to rest. The enforced layoffs immediately before big tournaments played havoc with my mind and my confidence.

During this time a personal trainer from the club where I was based in Buckinghamshire came to New Zealand. Vince was an ex-SAS instructor and quite a character. I had done a few 'Wince with Vince' sessions in the UK. He needed a job so I introduced him to a friend at Les Mills. Vince became one of New Zealand's first one-on-one personal trainers and I was his first client.

Vince introduced me to rest — a word that had been forbidden in my vocabulary and mindset. What Vince did not know about squash I taught him, and he opened my eyes to a whole new way of training. Above everything else, it was fun.

He travelled with me, and we marked out squash courts in

the sand on the beach, and did circuits through the forests. I appreciate now that my new regime outside the confines of four walls and sterile gyms was liberating.

While writing this book I found out that Vince took his own life a couple of years ago. I was shocked and saddened. We had lost touch when I moved out of Auckland. Why do we lose touch with people who have had such an impact on our lives? I just assumed he had got on with his life. Vince took the grind out of training and made it fun. I wish I could have helped him.

MY *ANNUS HORRIBILIS* WAS THE catalyst to the new Susan Devoy.

It had taken personal tragedy to convince me that something had to change. Now I had the opportunity to take all the adversity I had endured and channel it into a whole new experience. I had always believed that a champion is only measured by their victories, but I came to realise that being a true champion is about experiencing failure and defeat, learning from it and coming back. I was grateful for another chance to show I was the best, and to retire on top. And I wanted to enjoy the experience.

Which brings me back to that day: 10 October 1992, and the World Championship final.

I played the best squash of my life; I had saved the best till last. Faced with what was at stake — the expectations and the pressure — I rose to the occasion, and I couldn't have been more proud of myself, or more relieved. That part of my life was done and dusted.

Announcing my retirement felt like the weight of the world

being taken off my shoulders. I didn't know at the time but I was pregnant again. I had actually suspected I was during the tournament but there were no physical symptoms so I thought it might have just been wishful thinking.

It was confirmed soon after and I couldn't believe my luck: all these amazing things happening at once. But I have always said you create your own luck, and John had certainly played a major role, especially as far as the baby was concerned!

A television crew had accompanied us and they got more news than they'd bargained for. That show aired on New Zealand television on Christmas Eve 1992. The producer, Robyn Scott-Vincent, also began ghost-writing my biography. No one will believe this but I swear it's true that I had never read it until I began the monumental task of writing this memoir.

Ironically, the last words in *Out on Top* are: *This is not the final chapter in the Susan Devoy story.*

It certainly wasn't. Even I could not have predicted what the next 30 years would bring.

Three
Starting
a Family

DISCOVERING I WAS pregnant was a fairytale ending to my squash career. It took away any doubt about my decision to retire. The next chapter in my life had been determined. There was no going back, and I could not have been happier.

I relished being pregnant. I bought maternity clothes and wore them before I even showed.

Deep down I was desperate for a daughter, but who says that openly to anyone? Of course having a healthy baby was all that mattered and we both told each other we didn't mind. But secretly, having spent my entire life surrounded by males, I had this underlying desire for a little girl. I know John was desperate for a son. We told them at the first scan that neither of us wanted to know the sex of the baby.

On 22 June 1993 John was getting ready for a sales trip to Kaitāia. I felt this funny sensation and I was suddenly standing in a pool of unidentified liquid. I realised that my waters had broken.

What now? I thought. I rang Tess, my midwife, expecting it would be like in the movies and we would be making a mad dash to the hospital. Funny how everything you learnt at antenatal classes goes flying out the door when the time arrives . . .

Tess asked, in her strong Irish brogue, 'Have you had any contractions?' I said no.

'Well, just hang on for a wee while and see what happens,' she said.

Patience has never been one of my virtues and each passing hour seemed like an eternity.

Eight hours later Tess decided it was time for me to go to hospital. Back then, National Women's was part of Greenlane Hospital and was where most women in central Auckland gave birth. The first private Auckland birthing centre had just opened down the road in Gillies Avenue and I was looking forward to a few days of luxury there after the delivery.

In hospital, still nothing seemed to be happening and my patience was wearing thin. Eventually they induced me by administering a hormone called oxytocin. Things started moving quickly then and I soon found out what a contraction was. *Geez*, that was painful, but in my typically staunch and stoic manner I refused any pain relief. I was determined to have a natural birth.

But seriously, did women really go through this? I had recently had a kidney stone and the male doctor told me the pain was akin to childbirth. It was bloody obvious he had never had a baby.

'There are no medals at the end of this for bravery,' Tess reminded me, and I didn't need much convincing. 'I'll take whatever you've got,' I eventually groaned between the contractions. At first it was gas, gas and more gas (a mix of nitrous oxide and oxygen).

Things were still moving along at a snail's pace — I was hardly dilated despite regular contractions. The baby was not budging. Tess said we were in for a long haul so John nipped home (i.e. he went for a run around Cornwall Park, a beer with the neighbours to update them on progress, and a quick trip to McDonald's for dinner).

When he came back I was in one of the fancy birthing pools. Tess suggested John might like to get in and rub my back ... My conservative, prudish husband looked aghast and matter-of-factly pointed out that he hadn't brought his togs. Meanwhile I was flapping around naked as a jaybird ...

By this stage the big guns were called in: my GP, the obstetrician and an anaesthetist all arrived to survey the situation. We were now well into the early hours of the next day.

I can't recall much except that I was exhausted. John tells me that he and all the male medical professionals were in the lounge watching television when Tess marched in and said, 'This baby has to come out.' Suddenly it was battle stations. John donned a gown and gumboots and was told he would be a father in about fifteen minutes.

It hadn't been in the original plan to have a caesarean, but once they realised the baby had passed meconium in the uterus it was all hands on deck to get that baby out. It's a weird sensation — you can't feel anything except this tugging sensation. John was down at the business end, totally overawed by what he was seeing. At one stage I heard him ask, 'What are those?' He was pointing at my ovaries, which he declared looked like sweetbreads.

And just as they had said, in a matter of minutes a baby was born. Julian John Gordon, named after both his grandfathers, had taken his time to enter the world but he looked like a perfect little angel.

I was transferred the next day to the birthing centre as planned. Honestly, I felt like shit and royalty at the same time. Within hours my room was adorned with cards and flowers — in fact the smell was so overpowering I woke in the middle of the night thinking I was in a funeral home.

My parents made the trip up. It wasn't their first rodeo — Julian was their sixteenth grandchild — but I was their only daughter, and Dad had had such a terrible year I knew this was special for them. He had recovered as much as he was ever going to from his stroke the previous year.

My mother was not backward in coming forward with advice on motherhood. Right from day one she offered plenty of tips on feeding, sleeping, bathing and even — believe it or not — toilet training. It was always her way or the highway, and more often than not I just went with the flow. It was easier that way, and besides, she had raised seven children so had pretty good credentials.

Mum was adamant that mother and baby should stay under virtual house arrest for six weeks but that wasn't going to happen. I wanted to get back in some sort of shape and having a C-section had put a bit of a spanner in the works. I had a date on a squash court and needed to impress the Sultan of Brunei, so lounging around all day in my dressing gown and slippers was not on the agenda.

In roughly eight weeks John and I and our new baby were planning to fly to Brunei. A few months earlier Jahangir Khan, the greatest squash player of all time, had rung out of the blue in the middle of the night. John had answered with a groggy hello.

'Hello John, it's Jahangir,' a voice said. John thought someone was taking the mickey.

'Excuse me, who did you say?'

'It's Jahangir. John, I coach the Sultan of Brunei's nephew on a regular basis. The Sultan has decided he would like his niece to get some coaching from the best, and I have recommended Susan.'

He asked John to send some recent magazine covers and articles, I suppose to prove my credentials to the Sultan.

John, who was by now well awake, asked about the mechanics of such an undertaking.

'You fly to Singapore,' Jahangir said, 'and the Sultan sends his private jet to pick you up. You will stay in a six-star hotel and wait each day to be notified of when your lesson is . . . say 4 p.m. for no more than an hour. The same thing will happen each day, and some days you might not get a call.'

'That's doable,' John replied nonchalantly. Meanwhile I am waving my arms and pointing at my pregnant belly.

Jahangir apparently said I would be showered with gifts —

watches and jewellery — over and above my daily fee.

'So, John,' he continued, 'what is Susan's fee? What shall I tell the Sultan?'

John is a master negotiator and I listened as he said to Jahangir, 'What do you get?'

Jahangir replied, 'I am different,' and of course he is. He is the GOAT (greatest of all time) of squash — a man with his face on a Pakistani postage stamp and on the livery of the national airline.

John plucked a figure out of the air. 'A thousand a day.'

'Dollars or pounds?'

'Pounds,' said John quickly.

There was no mention of the impending baby, but Jahangir's final comment was: 'One more thing — you must not tell anyone!'

Once Julian was born, we contacted Jahangir and agreed on a visit in August. It was a major undertaking travelling overseas with an eight-week-old baby but John and I were always up for adventures, and this had the potential to be a real winner, especially financially for the future.

MOTHERHOOD WASN'T EXACTLY A BREEZE. Julian was a beautiful but weedy little thing who didn't eat — or sleep — much. My mother thought I was completely bonkers going overseas so soon. Secretly I suspect she was angling for an invite to come along as the babysitter. *Not going to happen*, I thought. She would have been more of a handful than the baby.

Julian was a few weeks old when I made my first trip back

home to Rotorua to proudly show him off to all the relations. I remember walking into the lounge and immediately noticing that Dad was yellow. I know that sounds weird but it was so obvious. I knew Mum was exhausted from caring for him and I didn't want to make her feel bad so I didn't say anything, just suggested we take him to the doctor for a check-up.

He was immediately admitted to Rotorua Hospital for tests. I was at home with the baby and the phone rang. The doctor on the end of the phone asked for my mother and I explained that she was at the hospital. She had been out having a coffee and probably a fag when she visited my dad. The doctor matter-of-factly said to me, 'Your dad has liver cancer. We can discuss the options, but there's probably not much we can do.'

The hardest part was giving Dad this news. When someone has lost the ability to communicate, everyone talks about them but not to them. He understood readily enough, and while he couldn't say so, we knew he wanted to come home to die. Once again Mum would be at the centre of this, but she would have a lot of family support around her.

I stayed for a few days and then had to travel back to Auckland. I told Dad I'd be back. He said nothing but had the look of a man who had had enough. He had fought so hard over the past couple of years and he was worn out.

He died that night, and I am writing this on the thirtieth anniversary of his death.

We were grateful that it had been quick, but it meant I wouldn't be flying out to meet the Sultan of Brunei anytime soon. We let Jahangir know we wouldn't be able to make it in August as planned.

'Don't worry,' he said, 'there will be plenty of opportunities. I will be in touch.'

A couple of months later he rang to say the Sultan's niece had taken up polo, so that was the end of that.

Some blessings come in disguise. Truth was I was struggling. Julian was a poor feeder and was not gaining weight. He had repeated ear infections and there wasn't much sleep going on for anyone. I was still getting the hang of this motherhood lark and also grieving over my dad's death, and ended up with the postpartum blues. Unprocessed grief doesn't go away — it just gnaws away inside you.

Most mothers want to breastfeed their baby and I was no exception. Aside from the beautiful feeling of attachment, it's easy, convenient and cheap. Mum wasn't the greatest advocate for breastfeeding. 'I had seven kids, you know. They were all bottle-fed and they turned out all right.' Mum kept ranting about putting Julian on a bottle.

You're so vulnerable as a new mother. It's all just so new and so foreign, and every step of the way you're wondering if you're doing it right or making terrible mistakes. However confident a person you are, there is this ever-present anxiety.

Thank heavens for Plunket and Karitane nurses. There was a cool haven just down the road from us where you could place your little cherub in expert hands and put your head down for a few hours. I so looked forward to those visits — I would feed Julian and then enjoy some uninterrupted shut-eye. We were lucky in those days — I'm not sure that level of support is offered for new mothers today.

These expert women suggested that, given all that had gone

on, it might be worth trying to bottle-feed Julian. So I did. I had given breastfeeding my best shot for three months and was sick and tired of beating myself up about it. He blossomed from that day on — finally started growing like a mushroom. It worked for both of us.

I started to feel as if I was getting my life back. I didn't get over-anxious when I left him to go for a run because he was thriving, and I was even starting to enjoy motherhood, probably because I was more relaxed and confident. I was getting fit again, which was so important to me. Exercise and fresh air have always been my natural antidepressants.

It passes, and each milestone achieved makes all the sleep deprivation worth it. You get in a groove and find your feet and your confidence. You get your life back, albeit in a very different shape — one in which you are responsible for another life.

We went away for a weekend with friends at Whangamata. John and I went for a jog and somehow I managed to fall over. I didn't think much of it until it happened again and I started to wonder about my balance. What was going on? I went to the doctor, only to discover I was pregnant again. Holy hell — Julian was only six months old! This wasn't part of the plan . . .

Baby Alex was the complete opposite to Julian — a bonny bouncy boy who thrived from day one. I'm sure it helps that you are less anxious the second time around. Two under two was busy, but a second child is certainly easier in many ways.

I had another crack at a natural birth but once again ended up having a caesarean. This time it wasn't quite as scary.

Alex was five or six months old when he became miserable and wouldn't eat or drink. A mother's instinct is strong and I took him to our family GP, who prescribed antibiotics. The next day saw no improvement, and by now Alex, normally such an alert and awake child, was limp and sleeping a lot. I rang the GP, who told me to take Alex immediately to his house, which was closer than his surgery. His wife was also a doctor. Everything after that seemed to happen at breakneck speed. She took one look at Alex and called an ambulance.

Somehow, somewhere, Alex had contracted bacterial meningitis — every parent's worst nightmare. We were told the first 24 hours were critical. We owe his life to the specialist doctors and nurses at Starship Hospital, to our GP and his wife, and to my gut instinct. Alex recovered and never looked back.

Life with two boys only a year apart was busy but fun. We bought a section and built a house and then — without any thought or planning — I was pregnant again.

Surely this time it would be a girl . . .

This time around I didn't need John to hold my hand at every scan or doctor's appointment. When I went for the first scan for number three, I clearly remember telling the radiographer I did not want to know the sex of the baby.

He was chatting away as he moved the scanner across my stomach, with me watching the screen. 'What do you have now?' he asked casually. 'I have two boys,' I said, to which he replied, too quickly, 'Oh, I have three sons too.' I could tell from his face that he knew he'd inadvertently given the game away.

I put it out of my mind, convincing myself it was easy to get it wrong so early and it still could be a girl. I didn't tell John, but the night before I was due to go into hospital for another C-section (booked well in advance this time) we went out for a bite and discussed names. A few options got bandied around, and they were always boys' names. One of us made reference to Josh Kronfeld, the All Black, and we eventually settled on the name Joshua — without even thinking about it, we had added another 'JO' to our tribe.

I did suggest to John that he might like to take matters into his own hands if we didn't want any more children. Bloody hell — men get off so lightly. He would never admit it but I knew he wasn't the slightest bit interested in having someone operate on his bits.

A friend of mine went to a psychic — and I seriously don't believe in any of that fortune-telling stuff — but I was blown away by the things she seemed to know about my friend's life, and intrigued by her predictions. So out of curiosity more than anything else, I went along.

She looked at me and said, 'I am hearing from your father. He says you are thinking of having more children. Don't! You will have another son and it will push you over the edge.'

Well, that's it, I thought. *If I'm not going to have a girl then there is no way in hell I am having another baby.* (John helpfully suggested I hunt around until I found a psychic who 'foresaw' that I would have a girl . . .)

Little did I know it was already too late — baby number four was on its way.

Prior to the birth I discussed with my obstetrician the possibility of having a tubal ligation. It was obvious to all the world that John and I were very fertile and his seeming reluctance to have the snip left me with no alternative.

Geoff Bye, my obstetrician, had become a bit of a mate.

He said, 'This is an important decision. Let's wait until after the birth in case you reconsider.' I knew that was not going to happen. Four caesareans and four babies were plenty.

When Jamie was delivered, John proudly said, 'Guess what, sweetie? It's another boy.' John has always called me sweetie or doll. It's a habit rather than any profound declaration of his adoring love, and it certainly doesn't reflect my persona. But it has stuck for 40 years.

Geoff asked me if I still wanted to have my tubes tied.

'What do you think?' I replied. 'And make sure you tie a bloody double knot.'

When I got home from the hospital the first thing my mother-in-law said was, 'Never mind, you're still young enough to try again.' She wasn't the only one who assumed I would be devastated at having another boy.

I had six brothers and no sisters, and now four sons and no daughters — who could blame me for feeling a little cheated? I often joke that's my punishment for all the terrible things I have said in my life about men. You feel selfish admitting that you desperately wanted a daughter. But in fact by the time I was pregnant with our fourth I was resigned to a houseful of males. And I adored my little boys.

ONE DAY IN MAY 1998, when we were alone, John said casually, 'There is some mail that needs your attention.' He handed me an envelope.

It was a letter from the Prime Minister's Office inviting me to accept a damehood. To this day I'm not sure what the right word is, so I just called it a knighthood — somehow that had a better ring to it.

I was blown away — it was completely out of left field. I had already been honoured with an MBE and a CBE; never in my wildest dreams had I ever thought I would be knighted.

Keeping quiet about it until the public announcement was the toughest part. I can't keep secrets — my sons often tease me about my big mouth — so this was quite the challenge. It was about a month and it was on the tip of my tongue so many times, but somehow I managed it.

Queen's Birthday weekend finally arrived, the honours were announced, and our family adorned the front page of the *New Zealand Herald*. It's a photo I cherish.

Next day was rubbish day and I was pushing the wheelie bin up the driveway. A couple of women walked past and one called out, 'That's no job for a Dame!' I chortled. 'I know, but the chauffeur and the butler have got the day off.'

People assume such honours come with a package of perks and privileges, but sadly not — or not for me anyway. In fact it was a little awkward. People would always ask what they should call me. I didn't expect to be called anything other than Susan but I did observe that if any Sirs were in the same company the question was never posed to them; they were always addressed by their titles.

The Sirs' wives get to call themselves Lady So-and-so but poor old John received no such title. Our friends joked for a while and called him Lady John. He didn't see the funny side. But it is a sexist and archaic system.

This was 1998, and two years later the Labour government

under Helen Clark abolished knighthoods and damehoods. I was the youngest person to be knighted since Sir Edmund Hillary, which registered with me when I went to a Dames' afternoon tea and noticed I was the only one there without a hat and pearls. I used to joke that in years to come I would be on the verge of becoming extinct. The honours were reintroduced by Prime Minister John Key (Sir John) in 2009 and I was relieved I would at last have some company.

For a while there was a flurry of activity and I was invited to a few high-profile events. One will remain a highlight of my life for a whole lot of reasons.

Dame Susan Devoy was invited to attend the APEC leaders' summit at the Auckland Town Hall. It was the first state visit by a US president since 1964 so it was a big deal for New Zealand. John missed the cut again, but it saved on the babysitting.

It was a grand occasion. I was seated with Sir Peter Blake and Lady Pippa, Sir Edmund and Lady Hillary, and the President of Brazil and his wife. I sort of pinched myself — who would have thought as a young girl growing up in Rotorua that I would ever sit in a room full of world leaders and other dignitaries? And of course there was that sexism again: all the Sirs had their other halves in tow while John was at home with the kids.

The most famous guest by far was President Bill Clinton. I wanted to shake his hand but this was definitely not one of those occasions where you just wandered up and said, 'Gidday Bill, I'm Susan from Roto-Vegas.'

I noticed a procession of people were being escorted to have a few seconds with the president — the poor guy hardly got time to eat his dinner. Never one to miss an opportunity, I spotted

Josiah Beeman, the US ambassador to New Zealand. I had recently sat next to Josiah at Sir Edmund Hillary's eightieth birthday. I sidled up to him and asked whether, when time permitted, he could possibly introduce me to the president so I could shake his hand.

Later in the evening he did. Josiah said, 'Mr President, this is Dame Susan Devoy. She is . . .' and then he stopped, and the pause was both awkward and embarrassing. I could tell his mind had gone completely blank. Then he blurted, 'She is New Zealand's most successful Olympic gold medallist.' My heart sank. I had never won any sort of medal — squash wasn't even in the Olympics. But neither of them probably even knew what squash was. Oh well. I would just shake Clinton's hand and jog on.

But that guy oozed charm and charisma. With a big smile he asked me how many medals I had won.

To put my response into context: I wasn't thinking clearly, I was noticeably overwhelmed by the moment, and I just thought, *Well, the president has told a couple of great big pork pies in his lifetime so what the hell.* 'Ten,' I said. I then realised how ridiculous that must have sounded.

Cool as a cucumber, Clinton sort of winked and said, 'Ten? Well, you must be the world's most prolific gold medallist.'

I was so embarrassed I virtually crawled back to my table.

THE HONOURS HAVE GIVEN ME the opportunity to meet some amazing people in my life. Very soon after I retired from squash I was invited by Prime Minister Jim Bolger to a dinner with

Prince Charles at Government House in Wellington. This was not one of the big gala dinners or garden parties, it was an intimate gathering with the air of a relaxed Sunday-night roast dinner, except that the guest of honour was the future King of England.

John and I were introduced, and the prime minister explained that I had recently retired. Charles asked what we were doing now, and we said we were looking forward to starting a family. He immediately replied, 'I hope you have a good time practising.'

We had quite an evening. Max Cryer played the piano, Dame Malvina Major sang, and the night developed into a good old singsong around the piano — with Prince Charles. At the end of the day, people are just people.

WHEN THE BOYS WERE LITTLE they didn't understand what being a Dame meant. All they knew was that Mum had some fancy medals that were quite good for dress-ups. One young friend was a passenger in our car and said to my son, 'My parents said your mother is famous.' There was a quizzical look on his face — I just looked like any other mother to him, so he followed up with, 'What is she famous for and what is a Dame?'

Before I could open my mouth my son proudly announced that his mother was famous because she was the best squash player in the world, and no one could beat her. To which another son replied, 'No one except Dad.'

The response to the second question was: 'I don't really know what a Dame is but that is what people call her when they want something.' The question is worth asking. Why did I get a damehood?

I have never found out who nominated me or who the kind folk were who wrote supporting letters. Anyone can nominate someone for an honour but you can't nominate yourself. Now that I have written numerous letters of endorsement for other people to receive honours, I am grateful that people considered me worthy. But I like to think that my sporting achievements were just a small part of it, because my contribution to the community was the important bit.

Over the years I have been well and truly recognised by my sporting peers and even my country with a raft of honours and awards. But at the end of the day I would much rather be remembered for being a champion person than a champion squash player. As proud as I am of my sporting achievements, they are a distant memory, but they gave me the opportunity to do some good stuff.

I loved the community aspect — and I still do. Perhaps it is in my DNA, given that my parents were altruistic. Growing up there was always something to fundraise for — the new squash club, which was practically my second home; the local Catholic secondary school. If there was a job to do, everyone mucked in and did it. If someone needed a helping hand you gave it, no questions asked. They were true Labour supporters and epitomised the working class of their time.

My parents called Housie every Thursday night at the Whakarewarewa hall from as far back as I can remember. My dad said when I was growing up, 'Never forget where you came from and never forget the people who helped you along the way.'

So I diligently scroll through each honours list announcement not just for the new Sirs and Dames but to see all the recipients who make our communities what they are, tirelessly contributing with no expectation of any recognition. I am always glad when they get it.

I don't wake up every morning and think I was a world champion and they made me a Dame and isn't the world a better place for having me. In fact, quite the opposite. I remind myself just how lucky I have been, and that it's time to pay it forward.

Sometimes I get a tad grumpy and feel a little taken for granted — often it seems the more you do, the more people expect — but there's not much chance of any of this going to my head, as I was quietly reminded recently when I checked in for an Air New Zealand flight.

I couldn't check in at the kiosk so proceeded to the check-in counter. The lovely young lady behind the counter asked for some identification and I promptly handed over my passport, even though it was just a domestic flight.

My passport doesn't have the title Dame on it but my ticket did. She looked at me and asked what Dame meant. I was too embarrassed to launch into an explanation so I said it was my nickname, and she proceeded to give me a stern telling-off. She would let me off this time but I was never to do that again.

AT 35, WITH FOUR SONS born within five years, you could say I had been barefoot and pregnant for a while. I was keen as mustard to get back into some physical shape but it wasn't easy finding the time. Running seemed the obvious choice and a small group of us mums would meet weekly, leave the kids at a crèche and escape for an hour or so.

I soon caught the bug again and set my sights on running a marathon, which required more training than a weekly run. Once I set my mind to something there is no stopping me, so I was either up before the birds or would run after the boys had gone to bed.

The Rotorua Marathon in 1999 was the obvious choice. Growing up, I had stood on the sidelines of many Rotorua Marathons wondering if one day that would be me. There was a bit of sibling rivalry as my brother Julian was also running.

I followed the training plan as closely as I could, and luckily found a training partner to share those long, gruelling (and boring) runs.

The day arrived — it's always the first Saturday in May. John and I had travelled with the boys to Rotorua. There was something special about being in my home town and plenty of supporters on the sidelines cheered me on. I knew I wasn't in the elite group but my fiercely competitive nature meant I was going to give it my all. I was aiming to run 3 hours and 40 minutes.

John followed with the boys in the car and every few kilometres they would stop and yell and cheer. Initially I found it quite motivating, but as time wore on I began to think, *God, what do I have to do to get a few minutes' peace?*

As we began to get close I realised I hadn't seen my brother — what I didn't know was that despite very little training he had been ahead of me all the way. Then I heard he had hit the wall and had stopped at Rotorua Airport, with 10 kilometres still to go. I was gobsmacked to hear he had lit a cigarette, opened a can of beer and virtually thrown in the towel before someone told him his sister was coming down the straight. That was all the incentive he needed and he took off again to narrowly beat me. I was peeved.

It was quite an achievement crossing that finish line. My time was 3 hours 45. A finisher's medal was placed over my neck and within seconds I had four young men crawling all over me. Life had quickly returned to normal.

A few years later it was the fortieth Rotorua Marathon and a group of us were turning 40 so took up the challenge again. This time the goal was to break 4 hours and we did, but only by the skin of our teeth.

I have always thought I have one more marathon left in me, but in the sixtieth year of my life it seems time is running out and physically it just feels impossible.

Time will tell whether I turn up on the start line for the sixtieth Rotorua Marathon in 2024 . . .

Four
The Halberg
Trust

LIFE OFTEN UNFOLDS through unexpected events changing our path when we least expect it. Two such moments had an indelible influence on my life.

When I was twenty years old I was completely engrossed in becoming the best female squash player in the world. When I achieved that, the priority became not just to stay there but to keep getting better. Planning for my future was nowhere in my mind at that age. I was consumed by the demands of my sport.

The first turning point came in 1988 when Susie Simcock, a well-known sports administrator and manager of many New Zealand teams I was part of, approached me to ask if I would speak at an event for the Muscular Dystrophy Association. The original speaker had backed out at the last minute, and I found myself agreeing to step in. Susie's husband, Jon Simcock, a renowned neurologist, was the association's medical patron.

The event was not a glitzy affair but it was deeply moving. Until that time I knew nothing about muscular dystrophy. It wasn't until Susie explained it to me on the way there, and I saw the families with children in wheelchairs, that it hit home. It was a glimpse into the devastating reality of this condition, which involves progressive muscular weakness. I had never before met children who were terminally ill or struggling with severe physical disabilities and it made me realise how much and how easily I had taken my physical abilities for granted.

The Hebbends stand out in my memory. They were a farming family from Taupiri and they had three boys, two of whom, Stuart and David, had Duchenne muscular dystrophy. Their story had a profound impact on me.

Later, when I returned to the UK, I found myself connecting with a group involved with cricketer Ian Botham's walk to raise money for child leukaemia research. Botham was embarking on a journey to walk the length of the UK, from Land's End to John O'Groats, for the cause.

Looking back, I realise that these two unexpected connections — my first real contacts with charity groups — shaped my life in ways I couldn't have predicted.

I am not sure it was exactly an epiphany, but these connections took my mind away from my own personal athletic goals and opened my eyes to new perspectives, setting a course I would follow for the rest of my life.

I knew the Muscular Dystrophy Association was desperate for funding, and also wanted to raise awareness, so I thought about re-creating Botham's walk in New Zealand, for a different cause. John thought I was bonkers. What athlete in the prime of their career takes time out for such a massive diversion? However, he also knew that the idea of retirement had started to form in my brain and I was looking to the future . . .

Interestingly, I have just read *My Dream Time: A memoir of tennis & teamwork* by Ash Barty, the world tennis champion who sent shockwaves through the sporting world when she suddenly announced her retirement in 2022. Her reasoning totally resonated with me, the only difference being that I wasn't a multi-millionaire at 25 . . . Most sportspeople do eventually work out there is more to life.

In the throes of training and competing you're so caught up in it and working so hard it's easy to forget that actually it's a real privilege. Caught up in this insular world you can lose sight of the fact that being born with a talent and then being given every opportunity to use it are not gifts afforded to everyone. Sure, my hard work and endeavour got me there, but while squash is not a wealthy sport I still got paid to do what I loved.

How many people get to say that? Not everybody gets to achieve their lifetime goal and not everybody gets to be a world champion. I didn't realise how lucky I was.

Selfishly, at the time I also thought taking a break to organise a charity walk might just be the catalyst for renewed enthusiasm for the professional squash circuit. Without wanting to blow smoke up my own you-know-what, I was enjoying a high profile in New Zealand, and this seemed like the perfect time to do this.

WELL, THAT WALK WAS UNDOUBTEDLY a defining moment for me. It changed my life and my view of the world. 'The Walk', as we simply called it, was a long time ago — 34 years in fact, and only people of my generation remember it. It was 1988 and we walked the length of New Zealand.

It's not something you drop into everyday conversation, but it did come up recently. In May 2023 I was approached to see if I would be keen to participate in a fundraising walk for a charity called Sweet Louise. I didn't know Louise Perkins personally but I remember when she died, and the charity was established in her name. It provides support to the families of women who are living with incurable breast cancer. Their campaign is called 'Walk 50k This May'.

Given that walking is my exercise of choice (and necessity) these days, I was happy to help. Bree Tomasel, the effervescent presenter from my time on *Celebrity Treasure Island*, was also approached. The idea is to walk the 50 kilometres over a month, but I suggested Bree and I do the walk together, in one day. With her media connections she could generate some publicity, and between the two of us we could probably raise some good money.

Even though I was fast approaching 60, the idea of 50 kilometres wasn't daunting for me. While we were walking, I casually mentioned to Bree and her partner Sophia that I had walked the length of New Zealand, and they turned to look at me as if I was telling porkies. I then realised that 'The Walk' had been before they were even born!

We knocked that 50 kilometres out of the park and helped raise some significant money for this amazing charity. I met and walked with women with incurable breast cancer. Those conversations are difficult at the start but I soon realised these women were making the most of what precious time they had left, and they were happy to talk about it. Walking 50 kilometres in one month was a mammoth challenge for some of them but they were all keen to support a charity that existed for them. I was reminded again just how easy it is to step up and help someone.

Sportspeople and celebrities are often asked to lend their name or their muscle to assist organisations trying to raise money. Social media has made this easier in some ways and more challenging in others. I am quite relieved it wasn't a thing in my sporting heyday. You'd be scared to breathe, knowing your every move could suddenly become public property.

So I stepped up and helped, and somewhere along the way I came to the realisation that it's not what you do for the charity, it's what the charity work does for you. There is this warm, overwhelming joy when you see what your small effort can mean to someone else.

'The Walk' raised over half a million dollars by covering more than 2770 kilometres over seven weeks. There were no ATM or EFTPOS machines back then so there was a lot of cash collected in buckets and a whole lot of cheques written.

There was a small core crew of us, and lots of people joined the walk for various sections. In the middle of the walk I took the night off to attend the Halberg Awards in Christchurch, as I was nominated for an award. We chuckled at the comment from a famous sportsperson who had walked with us that day. Susan Devoy wasn't walking the length of New Zealand for charity, she was doing a pub crawl and getting paid for it!

I'm not sure how it happened, but we often finished our days at the local pub on the main drag of a small town. We would be the talk of the town and there was no shortage of people wanting to shout us drinks. The hospitality was simply amazing — Kiwis showing their great spirit and generosity. It was certainly one of the highlights.

Part of the magic of the walk was undoubtedly the families that joined us. The Hebbends took some persuading but eventually came on the entire walk. Thanks to the generosity of our sponsors they had their own campervan. It was amazing to see them have this wonderful family experience; it was also a daily reminder why we were doing this.

One day in the middle of nowhere with no one around (which seldom happened), I was pushing Stuart in his wheelchair and he needed to go to the toilet. He was sixteen and I was 24 and I don't know who felt more embarrassed. It was a tough moment. I lifted his slight frame, and we muddled our way through.

After that it was just like we all had this beautiful understanding — it's hard to describe. We were like family. Other families with children with muscular dystrophy joined us, cherishing every day, as they knew they were not going to see their children grow up.

In the next few years I attended the funerals of both David and Stuart Hebbend. Then Don, their dad, died of cancer. I struggled to comprehend how a man who had taken such wonderful care of his boys could be punished like that. Where was the fairness?

TWO-THIRDS OF THE WAY THROUGH 'The Walk' we left my home town of Rotorua and were walking through the Mamakus when we noticed a helicopter landing in a clearing. As if in a puff of smoke, Sir Murray Halberg appeared out of nowhere. I was well aware of who he was, and of the work of the Halberg Trust, so it was quite a moment. I was even more slightly overcome when he presented us with a cheque for $5000. But there is no such thing as a free lunch, as they say. The catch was a request that I consider becoming a Halberg trustee.

I was not entirely sure what a trustee was, but I was humbled to be asked and happily agreed. 'You mean I had to walk all this way before you asked me?' I cheekily said.

In Robyn Scott-Vincent's biography I was quoted as saying:

My goal now is to see every child in New Zealand with a disability take part in active recreation or leisure on a regular basis. Kiwisport is a programme bringing a variety of sports to able-bodied young people and I would like to see that set up for children with disabilities.

Over the next twenty years that goal became a reality, thanks in large part to the efforts of Sir Murray Halberg.

Murray Halberg was a middle-distance runner who was born in Eketāhuna in 1933. After placings in several Commonwealth Games events and the 1956 Olympics in Melbourne, he won the 5000 metres at the 1960 Rome Olympics on the same day Peter Snell won gold in the 800 metres.

He established the Halberg Trust in 1963, a year before I was born, to support children with physical disabilities to be active in sport, recreation and leisure. He had a disability himself, in the form of a withered arm, after a severe injury in a rugby game in his youth. In 1988 he was knighted 'for services to sport and crippled children'.

I had never been on any sort of committee and was not offered any formal training as a trustee, which is not to say I wasn't offered lots of advice. Normally a person who has plenty to say, I initially found the trust meetings quite intimidating. I was the first female and the youngest by a long shot. Surrounded by much older men, mostly professionals and well regarded around the traps, I often felt out of my league.

But it was clear that Sir Murray had gathered around him some outstanding humans — gentlemen I came to love and respect as if they were my own father. Bernie Bookman had promised himself when he came back from the war after seeing friends killed that he would do something good in his life. Leo Hendry was one of the first members of the Eagles Golfing Society, a charitable institution that still supports the Halberg Foundation, as it is known today. They were good men and real characters.

For decades the Halberg Foundation has administered the Sportsman of the Year Awards, which is the charity's major fundraiser. When I won Sportsman of the Year in 1985 — before I became involved with the Halberg Trust — it was a memorable evening in more ways than one. My family of course were out in full force. Unaccustomed to fine dining — or should I say small portions — my brothers disappeared during the guest speaker to visit a fish-and-chip shop in Queen Street.

Later in the evening, when everyone was in good spirits, I was approached by some businessmen who owned a sharebroking firm in Auckland and wanted to sponsor me. Luckily my manager (aka husband John) was on hand to handle the negotiations. They offered me $15,000, which was quite a pot of gold in 1985.

John met with them the following day and agreed to invest that money in shares in the hope the pot would grow. We had never dabbled in the sharemarket but it seemed like the obvious thing to do, with all that expertise on hand. Fast-forward two years to the 1987 sharemarket crash and . . . well, you can guess the rest.

Players in minority sports like squash generally only get a look-in at the sports awards if it isn't an Olympic year, or a year in which a national team has won a rugby, cricket or netball world championship (or an America's Cup year).

None of those featured on the calendar in 1985 so I reckoned it was now or never for me. I'd managed to win another handful of 'sportswoman' of the year titles but never the big one, despite achieving the same results year after year. And, as it turned out, the award was mine that year.

The trust was evolving and, not before time, major change came to the naming of the awards. Given the number of women now in the running for the major award, it didn't seem appropriate to keep calling it Sports*man* of the Year. Mary Baker, mother of rowers Erin and Philippa, both exceptional athletes, would write to the trust each year to articulate her disgust at the archaic title of New Zealand's pre-eminent sports award.

I totally agreed but I was still the only woman on the trust, and Murray himself wasn't in favour of change. But I think my having won the award meant I carried some clout and eventually common sense won the day. In 1987 the awards title changed to the Halberg Awards, with a Sportsman of the Year, a Sportswoman of the Year, and a Supreme Award (as well as other awards). Murray Halberg wasn't sexist but he was a humble man who no doubt felt uncomfortable having the whole thing named after him.

This was the start of a paradigm shift for the trust as the benevolent group of people raising money for 'crippled children' morphed into an organisation intent on making enduring positive change for young people with disabilities.

No one today would ever use the term 'crippled children'. One thing I have learnt is that terminology is changing all the time and what was acceptable once might not be today because we know more. It's not 'political correctness gone mad', it's progress. But some were more willing to change than others. The key was to convince Murray; such was his mana that everybody came on board once he had made up his mind.

The transition was not rapid: we all had good intentions but we were all also volunteers with jobs and families, and we knew that a group of passionate volunteers could not take the trust to where we wanted it to be.

The discussion around employing staff was heated, as was the decision to buy a computer! I recall one trustee quipped, 'It's a shame a computer can't make cups of tea, then we wouldn't need women.' It was an uphill battle.

After I retired from squash in 1992 I had the time to become more involved with the trust and I was soon appointed the Auckland chairperson. Chairing meetings was a whole new ballgame but I was given excellent tutelage by the senior members (still all men). I didn't know my motions from my resolutions, but they all steered me in the right direction. Without even realising it, I was learning the ins and outs of governance. I was also seeing exemplary leadership in action, notwithstanding they were 'old school'. I found some of their views archaic, but they were all men of principle.

In 1994 we employed our first chief executive and a part-time administrator, which took the trust to a whole different level. Dave Currie, our first CEO, was a visionary — you just know when you meet someone who is ahead of their time. His plans were bold and brave, and he was passionate. We were navigating new territory and not everyone embraced that change, but Murray was totally on board and so we moved forward.

Currie had big ambitions for the trust and these required significantly increased funding, so it was all hands to the pump.

When I became national chairperson of the trust in 1995, I had a one-year-old, a two-year-old and another on the way. While searching for photos the other day I came across a handwritten note from former cricketer and broadcaster Iain Gallaway dated 12 March 1995, addressed to 'My Dearest Susan'. Iain and I had become great friends and he particularly enjoyed the company of sportswomen. In his note he joked he had missed me at the recent dinner but said his number two girlfriend, cyclist Sarah Ulmer, had been there.

He proceeded to ask whether I would be interested in chairing the Halberg Trust, though he did acknowledge that having two young children might make it difficult. He wrote: 'We are very much needing a charismatic chairperson with elite sporting abilities, and I believe that you would be an inspirational choice. Signed affectionately as always, Uncle Iain.'

How could I say no?

Murray's name and reputation in the community meant our list of trustees read like a who's who of New Zealand sport. Now it was time to spread the net wider.

The trust's flagship Halberg Awards were about to be given another shakeup. Guests had become accustomed to a black-tie dinner, predominantly attended by men who enjoyed a slap-up dinner and a guest speaker, followed by the awards ceremony. They were not televised back then so it was a small audience and a somewhat dated format.

Dave Currie took the annual Halberg Awards dinner to a whole new level — professional, entertaining and a real tribute to the winners. Most importantly, he got TVNZ on board and suddenly we got the awards out to the whole country, with an unparalleled opportunity to showcase the work of the trust. As board members we sometimes thought his ideas were crazy — fantastic, but crazy. How could he pull this off? But he did; they were giddy times.

In 1995, when Team New Zealand won the supreme award in an America's Cup year, he had their boat front and centre at the Convention Centre in Wellington. Even the mayor of Wellington at the time was in disbelief — how was that even possible?

One year a venue was erected in the Viaduct on the Auckland waterfront. It was exceptional but not waterproof — the punters at home watching on telly wouldn't have noticed but some of our guests got a little wet. Apologies were sent to paying guests. Someone replied telling us never to give up having good ideas.

But the *pièce de résistance* was in 1999 and a celebration of the sporting achievements of the decade. Dave had this brilliant idea to construct a venue outside the Auckland War Memorial Museum. The sticking point was the RSA, who were not overjoyed at the prospect. Cunningly, Dave wheeled Sir Peter Blake and Sir Murray to the crucial meeting and the RSA representatives were so overwhelmed in the presence of sporting royalty that the deal was signed there and then.

The ticket price for this event was astronomical but it sold out immediately.

At the event Sir Peter Snell was judged New Zealand Sports Champion of the 20th Century. Twenty years later my eldest son Julian would run a sub-four-minute mile to earn his Sir Peter Snell baggy cap at Cooks Gardens in Whanganui, the running home of Sir Peter Snell.

Lunches and dinners held around the country continued to raise significant funds for the trust. One year I travelled the country on a tour with Sir Paul Holmes and Sir Richard Hadlee. We had a lot of laughs. Paul was one of life's characters and we became good friends. He had always supported my career and was a generous and funny man who hosted some great parties.

As well as raising funds, these events helped spread the goals of the trust. Back in those days, long Friday lunches were popular and not frowned upon the way they are in some circles today. The Eagles Golfing Society organised golf days to fundraise for the Halberg Trust, and taking a day off work to play golf could be described as a charitable act.

So we had a successful formula for generating revenue. The key now was to spend it so it would have a lasting impact.

Dave was instrumental in bringing together a number of disability sports groups and, although I am certain he himself would be more modest, I believe this was a catalyst for the establishment of the paralympic movement in New Zealand.

We also launched Halberg Sports, the first programme the trust delivered, which became hugely popular as an after-school programme. The trust and its work went from strength to strength, underpinned by its 'No Exceptions' policy. This was ground-breaking stuff and I loved every minute of it. It had so much meaning and purpose and was the perfect role for me to combine with motherhood.

As I kept on having children they tagged along to events and functions where it was appropriate. This meant they grew up around people with disabilities and therefore never developed any prejudice. They didn't know any different.

I used to always say, 'Team, we are going to see children who are the same as you, but it's a bit tougher for them to do some things. They may also look different, but we're just trying to help them enjoy the same things you do.' Most of it went over their heads but they just mucked in on all the activities with the other kids.

I would always tell them that if they felt uncomfortable or awkward around someone, they should just look them in the eye and smile. It is human nature to stare.

This backfired once when we were down at the Viaduct Basin collecting for the Muscular Dystrophy Association. As per usual whenever we were out, the boys wanted something to eat, so were queuing at the counter. In front of us was a very large woman. Alex had that awkward uncomfortable smile on his face.

He only came up to her knees so possibly felt quite intimidated. Suddenly there was a loud beeping noise which turned out to be her pager (this was before cellphones). Alex promptly yelled: 'Watch out, she's reversing!' Oh my God. Among the giggles from other people, I was relieved that the poor woman had the good grace to laugh.

Dave Currie would often pop around to our place to get something signed or to discuss matters. We were chatting about it recently and he conceded our household at the time was chaotic.

When he was about four I took Jamie to the Homai school for the blind. Once again we discussed it beforehand, but Jamie didn't really notice too much different when he got among the young kids. After that we had to visit Dave at the Halberg offices. Dave had a visitor who was blind — what were the chances? I introduced Jamie, who just threw his hands up in horror and said, 'Not *another* blind person!' Thankfully, we could all see the funny side of that.

We teamed up with the Hillary Commission, now known as Sport New Zealand, and piloted a programme with Sport Bay of Plenty to employ the first sports opportunity officer. At that time of course I had no idea that in just a few years' time I myself would be CEO of Sport BOP. The pilot was so successful that these roles were introduced into all regional sports trusts.

I would have happily carried on my Halberg work forever. Not only did I love it, but it opened up other governance opportunities in both public and private sectors. While I enjoyed being at home with the boys, I knew I also needed the stimulation of adult work and adult company.

When I took up a full-time job in Tauranga in 2002 we ended up moving there. I carried on my Halberg work for a time but it was too hard. I had no free time, and there was no such thing as virtual meetings back then, so reluctantly I resigned. I couldn't do justice to the role and for a time it broke my heart.

But such great memories — and what a legacy.

I didn't miss too many Halberg Awards after I stepped down. The highlight was catching up with old friends, trustees now getting on in years who had taken this young female whipper-snapper under their wing so long ago. Sir David Levene wasn't a trustee but was probably the most generous benefactor over the years. He had a wicked sense of humour and he and many of the other wonderful trustees had become such great friends. The dinners were always like an annual reunion. Over the years all these people have passed away. In many cases Covid meant we never got a chance to say goodbye.

There has been controversy around the awards, especially in relation to how winners are determined. Why is someone who wins a world championship not as worthy as a gold medallist at the Olympic Games? If a team wins their world championship in the same year as the All Blacks win the Rugby World Cup, it's obvious who will win the supreme award because rugby is our national game. It doesn't necessarily mean theirs was the best performance on the world stage. And how do you choose between gold medallists in cycling and athletics?

I was judge for a time but gave it up — it's just too hard. And of course because I played a minority sport I was always pushing for the non-traditional sportspeople to be recognised.

At the end of the day it sometimes looks more like a popularity contest, but that's only my opinion. Sportspeople who may have been overlooked are usually fairly philosophical — their goal is to be the best in the world in their sport, and winning the Halberg Award is just the icing on the cake.

An alternative would be to have no awards and that would be a travesty. Irrespective of who wins, the awards ceremony is a celebration of all New Zealand's sporting achievements throughout the year. For a small nation we have for decades punched well above our weight, and long may that continue.

Five
My First
Real Job

WHEN I RETIRED in 1992 to start a family, life was sweet. Squash hadn't made me a millionaire, but it had given us a good start.

In my playing days John was my manager, a dab hand at negotiating deals and contracts. I was — and still am — completely inept at such things, so it was a perfect match. I just concentrated on winning and it turned out I was pretty good at that. We both knew it wasn't going to last forever, so towards the end of my career John went into a sports goods distribution business. His skills are in sales and marketing and an opportunity came up with one of my sponsors to become a partner and grow the business. With John loving sales and sport, this was a match made in heaven — or so we thought.

In the beginning he spent long hours on the road, travelling the length and breadth of the North Island. I would chuckle when he left, suitcase in tow, with his bag of tricks, as I called it. We would take bets on how much stock he could offload. He was a born salesman and loved the challenge.

John worked his butt off in those early years, and when we started having children the long hours continued; he would often catch up on paperwork when the kids were asleep. Neither of us is afraid of hard work, and if there is one message we have instilled in our children it is that there is no substitute for hard work.

Business was good and the company grew into a very successful operation. Life was sweet. Despite the long hours the business was growing. But not long after moving into new purpose-built premises, the red flags began to appear. Creditors hadn't been paid — how can a profitable business suddenly not pay the bills?

Stock also wasn't arriving and yet there was always a plausible-sounding reason that both John and the board accepted until it was too late.

By the time John realised the enormity of the situation, in 2001, the only option was to put the business into receivership. It was inconceivable to me that this could happen; my mother had just passed away and I was beginning to think that we were cursed.

I knew John had had no hand in this so I began a crusade to find answers. I was angry and hurt, but above all else I felt betrayed. How can someone do that?

What outraged me most was that the person we felt sure was responsible just disappeared. No explanation, no accountability

— he just walked out and left John to face the music.

I was furious and I couldn't let it go. I was also angry at John because he didn't want to go and smash the guy's lights out. At times like this our different personalities show their true colours — I wanted to exact revenge while John was resigned to moving on as best he could.

One night John and I got together with a former staff member who felt the same way as we did. We met at the Horse & Trap pub in Mt Eden to plot. We wanted to personally front up to this man and tell him how we felt, so after sinking a couple of stiff gin and tonics we went and knocked on his front door. He barely had time to open it before I stormed into his house, full of rage and contempt.

He just sat there while I hurled abuse at him. He offered no apology, no explanation, nothing. Just sat there staring at the floor. I had been advised to record the conversation but in the heat of the moment I forgot to turn on the recording device in my handbag, so I weirdly excused myself to go to the toilet. Later when we played back the recording of the rest of the 'conversation' all you could hear was my voice exploding all over the place.

His silence didn't provide much evidence, but we engaged a lawyer anyway and we went to the Serious Fraud Office. Nothing was going to stand in the way of my seeking justice. But after some time our lawyer sat us down and told us some home truths. 'Look,' he said, 'you will spend a year of your life and a truckload of money — for what? Even if there is a prosecution there won't be any money. He will go bankrupt. Do you really want to put yourselves through that?'

While I didn't think it at the time, I know now he was right, and I came (eventually) to appreciate the valuable advice.

Bad news always travels quickly and when word got out, a journalist rang me. I was pissed off — I was married to one of the owners but personally I had nothing to do with the business. Why call me? I was in no mood for a conversation but he kept badgering me, implying we had lost everything and couldn't put food on the table for our children. I said something along the lines of you needn't worry, mate. We're not living in a motorcamp in Papakura yet.

The next day's front page reported that Dame Susan Devoy's husband's business had gone bust, and Dame Susan had quipped that the family were not yet reduced to living in a caravan in the Papakura motorcamp.

Well, that opened up a Pandora's box. Abuse flooded in from all corners and the mayor of Papakura called me to ask for a retraction. So I wrote a letter to the editor quoting former US vice president Hubert Humphrey, who once said, 'Oh gosh, I wish I hadn't said that.' Then I said, 'To all those people who live in motorcamps, I am sorry; to those who live in Papakura, I am very sorry; and to those who live in motorcamps in Papakura I am very very sorry.'

I can't help my sarcasm; someone once described it as blunt humour with heart.

The *Sunday Star-Times* editor rang me to say my letter had won letter of the week and they were sending me a Waterman pen. To which I replied, 'Mate, you can stick your pen where the sun doesn't shine.'

We went from keeping up with the Joneses to simply keeping

up. Our Remuera house was put on the market and we moved into a rental. Some mornings I just wanted to pull the covers over my head and pretend this nightmare wasn't happening. But four young boys put paid to that. Anger and bitterness engulfed me. We were good people — what had we done to deserve this?

I got completely caught up in seeking justice — or at the very least accountability, or an apology, or anything rather than cowardly abandonment, leaving John to front the entire chaos. Caught up in my emotions, I failed to see how devastating this was for John. It had crushed him, but he hid it. While I wanted him to fight tooth and nail to get even, all he was concerned about was providing for his family. He hid all his emotions, to protect us and assure us that everything would be okay. He is an eternal optimist, and I am by nature a pessimist.

When you have four young children you have to carry on. John immediately took a new job, way below his experience level and capability, not to mention salary, but he was ready to do anything that would pay the bills, in the hope that eventually he would secure a better job. He is old school — he sees it as his responsibility to provide for his family and he was going to do that come hell or high water.

THE NEXT OPPORTUNITY TAUGHT US some good lessons in life. As Canadian author Malcolm Gladwell wrote in his book *David and Goliath*: 'Courage is not something that you already have that makes you brave when the tough times start. Courage is what you earn when you've been through the tough times and you discover they aren't so tough after all.'

When I was finally able to put everything into perspective, I realised that if this was the worst thing that was going to happen in our lives, perhaps we were blessed after all.

The turning point was when someone sent me the job ad for the role of CEO of Sport Bay of Plenty. Until that point it had never occurred to either of us that I could become the breadwinner of the family.

I had never been to a job interview, but how hard could it be? While I knew nothing about running a small business, there wasn't much I didn't know about sport. Thankfully I have the gift of the gab, and I was about to learn what 'fake it till you make it' really meant.

When I got the job, at the end of 2002, we packed up and moved the whole family to Tauranga. On my first day in the job I went to my office in a grungy building on Cameron Road, near the centre of Tauranga. I shut the door, turned on my computer and honestly thought: *What do I do now?* Here I was at 38 years of age setting out in a whole new direction.

Early on, a woman made an appointment to see me. Paula Thompson had until recently been CEO of the Tauranga District Council and now had gone out on her own as a business consultant.

Paula generously and genuinely welcomed me to the city and said how great it was to have me there. She told me a little bit about herself and offered to help if I ever needed anything. She remembers me asking whether she had come touting for business. I am sure I wouldn't have been that rude!

Pretty soon the honeymoon period was over and the enormity of the job ahead was dawning on me. John was a valuable resource — every night after work I would bombard him with questions.

I had stepped into an organisation that had recently undergone a major restructure. I have since learnt through experience that restructures, no matter how positively they are framed or sold to employees, are usually a sign that things are not good financially. Of course there are organisations that restructure to boost productivity or find ways to do things more efficiently, but in my own experience it's always been about the costs — and unfortunately usually involved human cost. My predecessor had done her best but there were massive expectations on me and my skeleton staff.

Regional sports trusts rely on funding — from central government or through Sport New Zealand, and from local councils, community trusts and gaming proceeds. We didn't have enough money or staff to achieve anything very much, and there were nights when I lay awake wondering how I was going to pay the wages. Aside from being a parent, I had never felt so responsible for other people's livelihoods.

Also weighing heavily on my mind was a deep sense of imposter syndrome. The staff thought I was this knight in shining armour coming to save the day but I didn't know how to do it. There's no denying I like to be successful, but I was so overwhelmed.

Just when I was beginning to panic, I think it was an employment issue that prompted me to ring Paula for advice. We organised a meeting, and once we had broken down the initial barriers and sussed each other out, there was an instant chemistry.

That meeting was the biggest break I ever got in my working career. Paula described my situation as raining cats and dogs — all these issues were pouring down and I hadn't found time to put up the umbrella. Step by step, she put me through what we coined the Winnie the Pooh school of management. As Christopher Robin said in the film *Pooh's Grand Adventure*, 'You're braver than you believe, stronger than you seem and smarter than you think,' and Paula made me believe it. She was my saviour — always at the end of the telephone or in my office helping me steer the ship. There was no ulterior motive, no hidden agenda, but man, I was suddenly on this steep learning curve with the best teacher around.

What a difference it made having someone like Paula in my corner. For no remuneration, she helped me build the capacity and capability of this small organisation and I felt as if I earned my business management qualification, even if it was from the Winnie the Pooh school of management. After our first year Paula presented me with a certificate signed by Winnie himself.

The key, I discovered, is to surround yourself with talented people. Good leaders are able to accept their own strengths and weaknesses and fill the gaps, and I recruited some fantastic individuals to work at Sport BOP, many of whom are still there today.

I did, however, at times circumvent normal business practice . . . My sons were attending St Mary's primary school and I was super impressed with the school's sports coordinator, Vicki Semple. Perhaps because Vicki was a mother of five sons, she understood the importance of sport and activity in kids' lives. I realised I wouldn't be popular at the school if I poached her, but I knew Sport BOP needed a presence in the local primary schools and Vicki was that person.

We both recall our first meeting/interview. Vicki asked me what her job description would be and I told her I didn't know but we would figure it out as we went along. I said her first task would be to meet with the local intermediate school principals. They had suggested starting up a middle (intermediate) schools national competition and needed some help from Sport BOP.

This was the start of the AIMS Games, today one of the largest sporting events in the country. The first year there were 700 or so competitors from seventeen schools and four sporting codes; now more than 10,000 kids from schools all over the country compete in multiple sports. Being part of something so amazing right from the beginning filled me with enormous satisfaction.

My son Julian ran in the inaugural cross-country, losing to a young boy called Mohamed Ali, a refugee from Djibouti. He was so talented but after a few years he dropped off the radar. I was delighted years later to meet up with him again when he was coaching a football team at an ethnic football competition I was involved with as race relations commissioner.

CoachForce was another jewel in the Sport BOP crown. It started in 1997 with five summer codes and five winter codes, and today eighteen codes are represented in this programme to create more and better coaches.

Miraculously I became good at securing funding. I say miraculously because I have always felt uncomfortable asking for money for anything, but I am good at telling or selling the story — those speech lessons Mum made me go to were put to good use. It's actually easy to talk about something you really believe in, and with any luck you inspire others to climb aboard for the ride.

THIS WAS WHEN MY LOVE affair with squash was reignited. I had barely entered a squash court since retiring and certainly had no intention of picking up a racket. John was still keen as mustard; he has always loved being active and competitive so he had quickly joined the squash club, and the boys naturally followed.

Squash clubs are still, as they were in my childhood, great places for kids to hang out, and with no pressure at all from us they all quickly became hooked. They loved whacking the ball around the court, and with four of them there was never any shortage of sparring partners. Soon their friends started getting interested and there was quite a little gang getting keener and keener.

The squash club in Tauranga back then was in an old, cold and dilapidated building. It was generally warmer outside than inside, and the facilities were dated, a fairly common scenario for a lot of squash courts around the country. The committee was already exploring opportunities for a new club. They owned the land and the building, but the land was no longer big enough for what they needed. The difficult part was finding somewhere to build that we could afford.

There were meetings galore with the local council, as well as feasibility studies, approaches to funders, plans, building consents. It was definitely a marathon, not a sprint. It's easy to become disillusioned when progress is so slow and this is how it felt at times, but the core group were in it for the long haul.

I have learnt over time that the success of any group depends on the combined strengths of the individuals, and the ability to utilise those strengths. And every project needs an ounce of luck. Successful community outcomes also depend on partnerships. At the time we were also looking for new premises for Sport BOP, and I was in discussion with various potential partners. What if we could find a site that could house a new squash club *and* Sport BOP?

Tauranga Boys' College had some land across the road from the college that had originally been earmarked for a boarding hostel. When the hostel didn't eventuate, they decided to gift the land to the squash club and suddenly the project had life. Except we weren't expecting the global financial crisis, which significantly reduced the value of the land we wanted to sell, so at the end of the day we were still a million dollars short.

The ounce of luck we needed came in the form of an interest-free loan from the Bay Trust. This was uncharted territory for the trust but it was a game-changer for the squash club and meant we could push the green light on building.

Amid great excitement, we managed to get the prime minister to agree to open the new building in 2011. John Key had, in his day, been a handy squash player out of the Burnside Squash Club in Christchurch, and I knew he would be the ideal person to open our new state-of-the-art facility. But it wasn't easy to organise. Initially I got no response from the PM's Office to my invitation. I persisted but couldn't get past the gatekeepers.

This called for lateral thinking. Quite by accident the PM and I had both been asked to present an award at the annual

Halberg Awards. We made our way on stage to make the presentation and, as we were leaving, I slipped him a note I had penned, virtually begging him to come and open our new club. I added my mobile number at the bottom of the scribbled note. He texted me immediately: 'I think we can make that happen.'

I am constantly astounded that we live in a country where our political leaders, our sporting and other heroes are so accessible. It's hard to imagine that happening in any other country.

The PM arrived on the day and was welcomed with the customary pōwhiri and haka from Tauranga Boys' College. After the official opening he got on court with the locals, engaged with all the young people and it was a huge success.

The Devoy Squash & Fitness Centre, as the facility was named, has gone from strength to strength, and having my name at the entrance fills me with pride. I'm constantly correcting people who assume John and I own the building, but I have to pinch myself sometimes when I wander into that club and realise that this is one of my legacies.

That aspect wasn't plain sailing. There were a few people who were opposed to the whole development and did not believe it was in the members' best interests. They threatened an injunction to stop the sale of the old club, and when the club was opened, those same people refused to play under the name Devoy Squash & Fitness Centre. If that isn't a case of tall poppy syndrome, I don't know what is. After all the work that was put in, none of which was for personal gain, their attitude really hurt.

I NEVER GOT TO ENJOY those lovely new Sport BOP offices because I resigned in 2006, after four years in the job. But those early years at the new squash club were fabulous. There was such a buzz around the traps as people came to terms with having this state-of-the-art facility, and the surge in membership reflected that.

It was so reminiscent of my own childhood. These facilities were a lot flasher but clubs are not just bricks and mortar. It was the environment and the people that brought back fond memories for me. It is still all about people and an environment that fosters sport and camaraderie.

I get such a thrill from seeing people enjoy the game that gave so much to me. In the beginning squash is not an easy sport to grasp, especially if you don't have natural hand–eye coordination, but with good support everything is achievable, and once you connect with the ball and have a few rallies then you are off.

The annual highlight for your average squash player is a teams tournament called the Super Champs, which allows players from beginners through to elite level to play in a teams event against other clubs across New Zealand. It is the jewel in the crown for the sport because it gives everyone a chance to be a champion in their own grade.

In the first year the new club was open I put my hand up to coach the F-grade women — real novices. They are the most rewarding and easiest to coach. Generally they don't know much, they're super enthusiastic and are like sponges, absorbing everything thrown at them.

At the beginning some of them had no idea of my squash

pedigree. It was quite hilarious when the penny dropped and they worked out that the name on the building was the same as the person coaching them!

My starting point is always you don't play squash to get fit, you have to be fit to play squash, so I introduced a boot camp and at 6 a.m. three mornings a week I put the women through their paces. It was open to anyone, and we had women of all ages, sizes and ability levels. If I was away John would substitute. The women were so grateful they sometimes brought dinner for John and the boys to say thank you.

I soon realised how many women there are who take no time for themselves. Between working jobs and raising families and volunteering for their children's sport or other activities there is almost no time left for them. Couple that with a lack of confidence and a dose of self-consciousness and they are filled with trepidation at either failing or being humiliated.

I took such pleasure in showing these women what they were capable of, and how getting a little fitter would mean they enjoyed their squash so much more. They were a special bunch of women who became the backbone of volunteers for our club. They surprised themselves with what they achieved and, above all else, it was a heap of fun.

Needless to say, our F-grade team went off to Nationals in Invercargill that year and obliterated the opposition.

Sadly, when I took up the role with the Human Rights Commission in 2013 I could no longer do it. I tried again when we eventually moved back to Tauranga years later but it was never the same. Age may have had something to do with that . . .

As I'm writing this I'm poring over old photos with John to

jog my memory, and neither of us can believe how we managed to fit it all in. Our four boys played every sport, starting with football (or soccer as we called it then) and swimming lessons (their mother's aversion to water made sure of that). Then it was rugby and basketball and volleyball and golf. Cricket was their summer passion — and of course squash. They took to everything with alacrity.

We were blessed and I suppose took it for granted. We were determined not to be those parents who exert too much pressure too young, but all four boys loved sport and gave it 100 per cent. Needless to say it was a huge thrill for us as their parents.

We lived a stone's throw away from the squash courts, which became the boys' home away from home. They had obviously inherited the genes from both parents and definitely got the bug. Just as my parents had done for me, John and I spent many weekends ferrying them to different tournaments around the country. Many of those squash buddies have become friends for life.

We tried not to think of the cost but they were expensive weekends. Not everyone was keen (or able) to accommodate our whole mob. John used to say it was an investment in their lives. I recall taking a big gulp whenever I paid the entry fees. John was playing too so I remember coughing up $200 one year for all of them to play in the Te Puke Easter tournament. Some tournaments offered prize money; I note that the boys never considered that they might like to repay their main investors . . .

When I accompanied them to squash tournaments I was just the boys' mum, but given my history it was difficult at times. There was undoubtedly an unspoken expectation that they would be good, and they were, but they came under tough scrutiny. This was particularly evident when things went badly and one of them spat the dummy. I always felt all eyes were on me, as if to say, 'Look how Dame Susan's boy is behaving!'

On one occasion when they were old enough to know better I drove three of them down to Hastings for the national champs. In the first match Jamie twisted his ankle. I suspected it was an excuse because he was obviously out of condition and didn't want to lose. Then Josh played and performed like a prize idiot, arguing with the referee. I went down between sets and told him to pull his head in. There was a heated exchange with some expletives that I will not repeat here . . . I just saw red, got in the car and drove back to Tauranga without them.

Poor Alex didn't deserve to be abandoned; he was never a problem. But he wouldn't have been perturbed by my leaving. The others knew better, or at least they should have. John was always saying I was too soft and never followed through on threats, so I rang him and told him I had this time.

I can't lump all the boys together, but Josh certainly kept us on our toes. He was fiercely competitive and a hothead. While he may have been right about the refereeing on that occasion that was no excuse to lose the plot completely. Such outbursts were often quite entertaining, but not if it was your child.

Thankfully he grew out of it — they all did — but it took a long time. When they say it's in your blood, it really is.

Julian is the only one who didn't keep playing squash. Running is his career and the risk of getting injured in squash is too high, but he enjoys following and supporting the others. John and I consider ourselves lucky to still be able to watch our boys play sport, whatever sport it may be and at whatever level they're at.

Golf seems to be the sport of choice at the moment and yet another passion they all share. John loves nothing more than a round with his sons on the weekend. (Despite telling me they need to be financially independent I note that he still pays their subs . . .)

The saying that a family that plays together stays together certainly seems to apply to us. Our boys' involvement in sport has brought John and me so much joy over the years.

Six
Raising
Boys

YOU CAN IMAGINE my relief, with four boys under five, when Julian started school in 1998.

Some mothers cry on their child's first day of school but I was ecstatic. The only anxiety I felt was about how the hell was I going to get them all out of the house on time. Our morning ritual was akin to herding cats, but I was keen to make a good first impression and somehow managed to make sure everyone had at least combed their hair and wiped the Marmite off their faces. John travelled a lot and worked long hours. He was usually home for the witching hour but most nights would go back to the office when the boys were in bed, and was up with the birds to go back to work. So I often flew solo in the mornings.

Julian started his school life at St Michael's Catholic primary school in Remuera. He had had a few school visits and was ready. I was more than ready.

His first day is etched in my memory. In one hand I was carrying Jamie, who was eight weeks old, in his car seat, while the other gripped the hand of Josh, who was well into the terrible twos. I was yelling at Julian and Alex to stay close.

So far so good. The school bell rang and Julian trotted off to start his new life. Another milestone was ticked off. We began walking up the driveway back to the car, a short steep stretch up to a busy road.

Suddenly without any warning Alex took off at lightning speed. I couldn't chase after him with the others in my grip and I was petrified he would run out on the road. 'Please stop him!' I screamed at the top of my lungs to the other mothers waiting at the top of the driveway. A kind mum grabbed Alex as he ran past. By this time I was in earshot and as he turned around I clearly heard him tell her to 'F... off!'

The women's mouths dropped to the ground. Some chuckled while others looked horrified. I was mortified. I apologised profusely and frog-marched Alex away as I felt my cheeks redden with embarrassment. Excellent. Day one, and the Dame's children had already made their mark.

Such memorable episodes aside, what amazes me now about that time of my life is how little I remember, apart from everything being busy and sometimes chaotic. In the blink of an eye I had three children at St Michael's. The mornings by then were more stressful as we had moved to Epsom and the trek through the Auckland traffic was a daily nightmare.

In late 2002, when I got the Sport BOP job, we made the

move to Tauranga in the sunny Bay of Plenty.

The boys were naturally reluctant to move. They felt sad about leaving their friends and nervous about starting a new school. In fact we were all apprehensive. The decision had in some ways been forced upon us and it was to be a major shift, in which I was going to work full time and John was about to become a stay-at-home dad.

Housing in Tauranga was cheaper than Auckland and we found a beautiful house to rent until we sold in Auckland. Then we bought a fabulous family home, so the move seemed like a grand adventure. St Mary's, the local Catholic primary school, was within walking distance, although I confess we drove a lot. It was just easier to bundle them all in the car than organise the walking school bus every morning.

Jamie was still at home and going to the Montessori pre-school across the road. This was one situation where our proximity did not help. The cunning little bloke knew his father was at home — he could look out of the window of the preschool and see him. Inevitably John would get a call to pick up a 'sick' Jamie, who much preferred being at home playing footy and cricket in the backyard to learning his colours or the alphabet. When you have four kids the youngest basically gets away with murder. You simply accept that his life will not be ruined if he hasn't quite mastered reading and writing before he starts school.

Some parents get sucked into thinking their child is an Einstein, and being pushed up a class or placed in the accelerant programme is considered some sort of status symbol. We decided to go the other way. Julian had been the youngest in his class in Auckland, and he was doing okay but he was so young and tiny. He was more than capable but shy and introspective.

With the move to Tauranga we had a chance for him to be put back a year, to give him an opportunity to shine. So we did. You never know at the time whether these decisions are right or wrong, but you learn to trust your instincts. You also learn every child is different. We thought Julian would do better as the oldest in his class, and it also meant we would have all the boys at the same school — albeit only for one year. We didn't always get the decisions right, but this one worked out well.

We had a big celebration when Jamie, the youngest, turned five. The few new families we had met in Tauranga joined with some old friends from Auckland who came down to mark the occasion. It was the end of one chapter and the start of another: all four boys were finally at school.

We hired a clown for the day but the boys soon exposed his shortcomings — he wasn't funny or entertaining and he certainly had no special tricks. When he came to leave he couldn't find his car keys and adamantly accused the boys of stealing them. We spent hours looking for them as the 'clown' became more and more irate. Eventually John had to give him a lift to Rotorua. In one of life's little mysteries, the keys were never found.

I HAD BEEN LUCKY TO have the time I did at home with the boys, but now I was plunged into a full-time paid job. It was tough yakka, but I had the perfect mix of work, motherhood, and my role as chair of the Halberg Foundation (which I continued for a short time after moving). I was also involved with other charities and was beginning to get some great governance opportunities.

The whole dynamic changed and it took some adjusting to. John and I had always said that if possible one of us would always be at home for the boys, but I never actually envisaged that it would be him!

John would be the first to admit he's not fantastic at domestic chores, and nor is he Jamie Oliver in the kitchen. Things I thought were no-brainers were foreign to John, like separating the washing into whites and colours. For a period all our clothes changed colour, sometimes more than once. I used to say to myself, oh well, if tie-dyeing comes back into vogue we'll be off to a running start.

The meals were edible but monotonous and I confess I became a bit of a nag around cleaning standards. It really is true that even when women work full time they often still carry the load of most of the housework and the organising. John won't agree but this is my book, and he has a short memory! Someone wise once said if you lower your expectations you won't be disappointed. I tried to adopt that attitude but didn't always succeed.

Walking from my office one day to get a coffee, I saw John in the café with a group of women. Bemused, I asked him about it later and he said he had joined the PTA. 'Great,' I said. 'Maybe they can give you some cooking tips!'

At the end of the day, the boys got to spend some real quality time with their father, and while it sometimes ground my gears at the time, I see that beautiful bond with their father still alive and strong today.

I HAVE NEVER THOUGHT OF myself as special or different from anyone else but if you have lived in the public eye, people sometimes make up their minds about what sort of person you are ahead of meeting you, which can make it quite difficult to adjust to a new community. My reputation is as a hard-arse or an iron maiden. I know it was tricky for John and the boys sometimes too. And sometimes I can't help giving as good as I get.

I was giving a speech once for Breast Cancer Awareness Month — a volunteer gig for a charity I'm happy to support. After my address I was standing with a group of women and one said to me, 'You know, I have never really liked you but I must say you speak well.' An awkward silence fell over the group. The woman concerned didn't seem to understand what she had said. So I turned to her. 'Do we know each other?' I asked. 'No,' she replied. 'That's good,' I said, 'because I probably wouldn't like you either.'

All four of our boys participated in the St Mary's cross-country the first year we were there. As I have mentioned, all inherited good sporting genes and a competitive streak, and Jamie, the new entrant, was eager to match his brothers' exploits on the day. Prior to his race Julian, Alex and Josh had each won a medal, so when Jamie came charging down the home straight in fourth place, with all of us cheering him on, he suddenly reached out to the boy in front and grabbed his shirt, pulled him back behind him and nonchalantly ran through the finish line proud as punch for bronze.

He was oblivious to the outrage of parents and grandparents on the sidelines, and John and I were mortified. But we could see the funny side as well — and it wasn't the Olympics. Then I heard the titter down the line — 'You know whose child *that* is. No wonder they are so competitive.' Without drawing breath I glared at everyone and said, 'They get their competitive genes as much from their father as from their mother. The only difference is their mother was better at winning.'

Jamie was disqualified and had to apologise to the other boy, and John and I apologised to the boy's parents and grand-parents. But the die was cast — those Oakley boys obviously had to be watched — it was winning at all costs for them. The trick for us as parents was teaching them the balance between winning and good sportsmanship. It was always a work in progress.

I recall getting a call from a parent on a Saturday morning when I was doing the regular sport drop-off. Julian and Alex were in the same intermediate school cricket team and playing at Blake Park in Mt Maunganui while I was across town with the other two.

'You'd better come over,' I was told. Apparently Julian had run Alex out without facing a ball and things had turned sour — Alex had picked up stumps and left.

There were tears and tantrums, most of them in the backyard but some on public display. John and I always drilled into them that it was okay to be disappointed but not to show it, meaning if you wanted to cry, go and hide behind a tree. Thankfully, they soon grew out of the tears.

I confess I wasn't always the perfect sideline parent, but I tried to keep myself in check. There were a few steely glares at coaches if my kids sat on the bench the entire game. I know kids' sport relies on volunteers. John coached numerous teams and was always fair — everyone got an equal opportunity even if our boys thought their father should show them some favouritism. The sweetest story was when a meeting was held at school with kids and parents interested in playing cricket. At the end of the meeting a call went up to see who would be interested in coaching. There was silence until Alex grabbed John's hand and held it up. 'My dad will!' he told the meeting.

It wasn't all sport — we endeavoured to bring out their creative side as well. They enjoyed strutting their stuff in school productions, tinkered with a guitar and we bought them a keyboard, but it was sport that was the constant in their lives.

Our large home in Harvey Street was nicknamed the Oakley Oval. Depending on the season, the backyard would be marked out as a rugby pitch or a cricket ground and was always abuzz with kids from daylight to dusk. There were makeshift huts in the trees and skateboard ramps in the driveway. Squash games were played in the lounge, and table tennis on the dining-room table.

Like all kids they staged talent shows to show off their dancing and singing skills, and had races down the stairs in sleeping bags. There were putting greens, bowling lanes and triathlons — we had a swimming pool also.

And of course there were lots of arguments and my main role often became that of peacemaker. Sometimes I was allowed to umpire or referee.

Luckily we had a big section and didn't cause too much trouble for the neighbours. Apart from when the boys constructed a projectile contraption that fired potatoes 200 metres down the road onto some poor unassuming man in his garden. There were many shattered windows from wayward cricket balls but they were mostly ours, and one visiting child shot a spear-gun through our new television. I didn't even know we owned a spear-gun.

In short it was mayhem, but I had grown up with six brothers so I thought it was normal.

NOT LONG AFTER WE SETTLED in Tauranga John was offered a great career opportunity. I knew he was desperate to get back into the workforce — being a househusband wasn't really his cup of tea — so he went for it. With both parents working full time and John's new job involving a lot of travel we had a very busy house. It sometimes felt like we barely had time to breathe.

For a while we had the most amazing after-school caregivers: two gorgeous young women who were studying to be teachers. Sarah and Rochelle formed beautiful bonds with our boys. To their credit they never complained, but I could only imagine the after-school mayhem they had to deal with. Various stories have filtered through over the years . . . I hope they know how much we appreciated what they did.

We even had the odd famous babysitter. During one school holidays rising cricket star Kane Williamson looked after our two youngest for two weeks. We thought four might be a bit much for a fifteen-year-old so we enrolled the older two in a school holiday programme. Josh and Jamie thought they had died and gone to heaven. Kane was a handy rugby player as well as a cricketer, so it was endless hours of kicking balls and throwdowns, punctuated by a few surfing videos.

Once John got established in his job we both decided it was just too much. I needed — and wanted — to be at home. I was proud of what I had achieved at Sport BOP but it was exhausting, and I felt I was missing out on too much at home. There was no quality time, and organising our schedules was impossible. Everyone's tempers were frayed. So I resigned, though I confess there were times subsequently, when things turned pear shaped, that I reckoned paid work would have been easier.

John was a saint. It didn't matter where he had been in the country or how long his day had been, the minute he got home from work he took over the kids. Not that he had much choice: I was virtually waiting at the door for him, saying, 'They're all yours.' But he never once complained or said no. He would take them for a swim at the beach, kick a ball for ages, or take them down to the squash club.

The highlight of each year for me was when John would take them all away for a weekend so I could have some peace and quiet. Even to this day my idea of heaven is being home alone. Off they would go to Rydges or a similar hotel in Rotorua, the prerequisites being a heated pool and a buffet breakfast included in the price. John would book a double room — two in each bed and Jamie on the couch or the floor. They would go to the maze, play mini-golf, soak in the hot pools and come home exhausted.

I would always ask John to have man-to-man chats with them about boys' things — you know, personal hygiene, the birds and the bees. I was sometimes quite specific in my instructions but don't wish to overshare here . . .

Lots of little gems have been divulged over the years about

those discussions. I was told that John would start off by saying, 'Boys, you know you need to respect girls and women . . .' A two-minute lecture would follow, to which the audience paid no attention and at the end of which John would breathe a sigh of relief. Job done. He primed the boys to say yes if Mum asked whether they had had 'the talk'. Another thing I heard was that John said to them, 'You boys are lucky you will always have three best friends.' They would ask, 'Who?' and their father would reply, 'Your brothers.' That warmed the cockles of my heart.

I once asked one of the boys how come they all loved John's old music. I was told: 'On our trips Dad always used to say, "My car, my music."'

WHEN JULIAN LEFT ST MARY'S we enrolled him at Aquinas College, a relatively new Catholic school for years 7 to 13. I am not a practising Catholic anymore, in fact not sure what I believe in. But I had been raised Catholic and sent to Catholic schools and I suppose I felt obliged to follow that path. I thought that smaller schools with special character would be better, and it was co-educational so they would get a female perspective from someone other than their mother.

Julian was an easy kid — quiet and quite introverted. We used to joke that as a baby he was an angel, so that's why we had a whole lot more. Initially he was happy at Aquinas, but increasingly I was not. The school was only four years old and still bedding in. There were no school camps, no school productions, and limited sporting options. I worried that Julian was missing out on important experiences. I got it that new schools can't have everything — apparently it takes around fifteen years to fully establish a school. My dilemma was whether I wanted my son to be a guinea pig.

It was a tough decision, but two separate events sealed the deal. One day Julian came home and told me that a certain teacher had said to him, 'Tell your mother that you should play rugby, a real sport.' Julian was a tiny kid and the suggestion was ridiculous. What's more, he didn't *want* to play rugby, but didn't feel comfortable saying so. I saw red. Then another day I turned up to pick Julian up from school and saw two students snogging right outside the school office. *Really?* I thought.

It's not easy making your child change schools but I trusted my gut. The other boys were following close behind so I needed to act quickly. And I did.

Tauranga Intermediate, just down the road, was the largest intermediate school in New Zealand and everyone I spoke to raved about the school and the remarkable principal, Brian Diver. My interview with him quickly dispelled any doubts I might have had.

Word soon got out we had left Aquinas — I got a call from a friend who had been playing golf with the bishop. Crikey, I thought, it's gone to the top! The bishop must have casually asked as they putted out the 18th, 'Do you happen to know why Susan Devoy has removed her son from Aquinas College?' I said to my friend, 'Why don't you tell the bishop to ring me.'

There was a lot of commentary around the traps, especially given that our other boys still attended the feeder school (St Mary's). But many parents sent their kids to other secondary schools. I note here that Aquinas College is a great school, but you have to do what you think is right for your kids at the time.

It proved to be the best decision we ever made with regard to our boys' education. All four of them would say their two years at Tauranga Intermediate were the best of their school lives.

Next it was Tauranga Boys' College. There is a fundamental shift when your precious young man starts high school, particularly a single-sex school. Suddenly we helicopter mums who have become accustomed to barrelling into the classroom to have a chat to the teacher see the barriers go up. The staff don't come out and say it directly, but you get the message. Hey Mum, we can look after your boy now and we would prefer it if you butted out.

Letting go is hard — your teenage boy still needs you, but not front and centre. You want to know everything but the more you grill him the more he clams up.

The saving grace for me as I navigated my sons becoming teenagers was reading Celia Lashlie's book *He'll Be OK: Growing Gorgeous Boys into Good Men*, and then going to listen to her speak. I was so impressed that I sent John another night. He was reluctant — he didn't share my anxieties about the boys, which is just as well. We didn't need two worrywarts in the family. He always believed they would be okay, and it turns out he was right.

John had no idea who Celia Lashlie was or what she looked like and when he arrived early at the hall he took a seat near the front. A woman duly sat down next to him and they got chatting. Asked why he was there, John replied that his wife had made him come. 'Apparently this Celia Lashlie is pretty good and I might learn something.' To which she replied, 'I hope so because I'm Celia Lashlie.'

He was also impressed by her and we both learnt something, namely that I was the one who had to change my behaviour. Lashlie believed that boys cross the bridge of adolescence between thirteen and eighteen, and that during that time mothers need to step back and play a less direct role in their lives. In other words, get off the bridge. What teenage boys need is a lot less molly-coddling from Mum and significantly more time with the good men in their lives.

Her words made sense but I found them hard to follow. The upside was that my boys had a good man in their father.

All through the years when the going got tough — and yes, we were tested on many occasions — I reminded myself that they would be okay. Now that they have grown into fabulous humans I hear myself repeating the advice to other mothers at the end of their tether with teenage sons.

ONE DIFFICULT ASPECT OF PARENTING for me has been trying too hard at times to ensure that the boys know they are all loved equally. We strove to give them all the same opportunities but even with the best intentions it just doesn't work out like that. One size sometimes does not fit all.

Family therapist Diane Levy once said to me, 'It's okay not to like them at times but you will always love them. You treat them all the same and yet they are so different.'

Our third son, Joshua, proved to be a handful from the moment he entered this world. Full of beans and with a wickedly cheeky grin, he was determined to do things his own way from the get-go, with little respect for authority, including his parents.

Josh was that kid you told not to cut his own hair and he did it anyway. The child who found the hidden crayons and proudly drew on the walls. The child to whom you said 'Don't touch' and he proceeded to destroy the entire shop display. He was a ball of unlimited energy, it was exhausting, and he was stubborn and wilful. He never knew when enough was enough.

It's tough when one child demands so much attention. Josh wasn't particularly keen on learning — what he loved about school was sport and his mates. I know that's not uncommon, but I worried that if he went to Tauranga Boys', where his elder brothers were trucking along, there would be expectations he would be the same, and when he wasn't, he would get lost in the system. So we explored the options with him and decided to send him to board at St Peter's in Cambridge. It was a difficult decision but as parents we felt it was the best thing for Josh.

Cambridge is only an hour away but it felt like the other side of the world when we dropped him off. He was a busy beaver for the first few days and there was no contact, but I immediately knew the honeymoon period was over when I was bombarded with texts. 'I hate it here.' 'I want to come home.' Adjusting to the routine of boarding life, the rules and structure, was just too much for him. It broke my heart.

Parents of first-time boarders are asked not to visit their child for the first three weeks while they settle in, so the first opportunity I got to see Josh was at athletics day. I expected from his texts to find this miserable soul, bereft and desperate, but I arrived to see Josh hoisted on another boy's shoulders wearing a grin from ear to ear. He also had a band-aid on his ear. After some gentle interrogation I found out it was an ear piercing, and I gathered Josh's handiwork had been applied to other boys in the boarding house. It certainly didn't get the tick of approval from the teacher.

After the first three weeks Josh came home every weekend. One of us would go and watch his Saturday sport and bring him home after. In the beginning it was hard to get him to go back after the weekend. He seemed paranoid that something was going to happen to us while he was not around. Despite our reassurances this went on for some time, so I made an appointment with a psychologist. I told Josh it wasn't a big deal but it might be good for him to talk to someone other than us about his concerns and how to manage them.

I waited in the car while he went in. I knew it wouldn't take long for him to start talking, despite his reluctance and obstinacy. Like his mother, he can't keep his mouth shut for long. Afterwards he told me the appointment had been a total waste of money and it was never mentioned again.

It didn't take us long to figure out that Josh was fine. He just wanted the best of both worlds — he enjoyed the camaraderie of boarding school but also didn't want to miss any of the action at home. Either way he didn't like schoolwork, but this way it was someone else's job to make sure he did it. That's what we were paying the big bucks for.

St Peter's was lucky enough to have its own squash courts and during the winter John and I made the return trip to coach the school team.

Meanwhile, back at the ranch, the other boys were getting on with life. I was too scared to ask them what they thought about Josh attending a private school when the same opportunity hadn't been offered to them. We couldn't afford to send them all. In a perfect world they would all have attended the local college and life would have been simpler. But there was less drama with Josh away. It was the right decision.

After three years at St Peter's, Josh decided he wanted to come home and finish his schooling at Tauranga Boys'. Our bank balance heaved a sigh of relief. Julian and Alex had both left home by then so there would be fewer feuds.

At this point we acquired a surrogate son — a young boy who wanted to come to Tauranga Boys' to play in the squash team. The college had a strong affiliation with the new squash centre in town and was the place to be for any aspiring squash player. His family were farmers from Reporoa, so Ben became our boarder. We must have been suckers for punishment as we did the same for another boy a year later.

A HOUSEFUL OF TEENAGE BOYS brings its own challenges. Another Celia Lashlie pearl of wisdom was that the best time for a parent to be around was after school. I assumed this might be about sharing their day but no, she said it was when they were plotting their next move.

And they were always plotting . . . well, at least some of them were. These angelic little babies were growing up before our eyes. Lashlie's book was my go-to bible for parenting teenage boys. She also said boys lied through their teeth, and she wasn't wrong. And they were not always those little white lies you could turn a blind eye to.

John took Josh and Jamie and a good friend of theirs down to Timaru for the New Zealand Junior Squash Open. It was Josh's last junior tournament as he turned nineteen the following week. They booked into a motel, and everything went swimmingly.

Jamie and his friend were travelling on to Invercargill with a crew on the Monday following the tournament, and Josh and John left to come home on the Sunday night. People might think we were crazy leaving two seventeen-year-olds to their own devices, but there were other parents staying in the motel, and the boys were given their riding instructions loud and clear. What could possibly go wrong on a Sunday night in Timaru?

We heard the next morning that they had made the bus so we assumed things had gone to plan. Then a few hours later we received an email from the moteliers with their version of events, including noise throughout the night and a smashed bottle of vodka outside the boys' room. Other occupants had complained.

Nothing was broken or damaged (apart from the vodka bottle) but it was embarrassing for us as parents. Jamie's friend's mother was on the same page and we were going to get to the bottom of it.

John was furious. He has a bee in his bonnet about alcohol, and especially about anyone supplying underage drinkers. These boys struggled to look fifteen so it was nigh on impossible that they had been able to buy it themselves. This wasn't our first rodeo: Josh had been in some pretty dire situations. We didn't excuse his behaviour — after all, he was the idiot who poured it down his throat — but John has no time for people who don't understand the consequences of supplying youngsters with the hard stuff.

We patiently waited for the boys to return from Invercargill to face the firing squad. And I have to hand it to them — both deserved Oscars for their performances. As bold as brass they told us some randoms had walked past their motel and dropped the bottle of vodka. We knew they were lying.

We said, 'The moteliers said it sounded as if you were up playing rugby all night.'

'That's not true!' they said. 'We were playing cricket.'

We got to the pointy end of the interrogation. We wanted to know who had supplied the alcohol.

There was deathly silence. Neither of them was going to dob anyone in. We threatened all sorts of punishments but they never budged, even to this day.

We had our suspicions, and I bet that boy was crapping himself about the wrath he would incur if John and Susan found out it was him.

You think they will learn from these life lessons, and perhaps eventually they do, but we were always on our guard. We wanted to give them opportunities to take responsibility and show us we could trust them, but sometimes they just couldn't help themselves.

The first time we left Jamie and Josh (aged fifteen and seventeen) at home by themselves for the weekend we drummed all the rules into them. No friends, no alcohol and no parties. They gave us their solemn assurances.

We had just arrived at our weekend destination when I saw a photo pop up on social media. The two of them were sitting in the spa pool with some mates, bottles of beer in hand. After a serious dressing-down on the phone I'm sure the boy who posted the pic got a lambasting. There were no more posts . . .

One morning I noticed a highchair in the driveway. Josh laughed, saying they had taken it from McDonald's, which was a late-night hangout for the local teenagers. I was furious. It may have seemed funny at the time but this chair was stolen property. He was to take it back immediately and apologise. Josh promised me he understood and that he and his friends would take it back.

The following day I was away but one of the boys rang me to say the police were at home questioning Josh. It transpired that Josh had returned the highchair, but with no apology. He just left it and headed for the hills, all of it caught on CCTV camera. The clever policewoman put the fear of God into him — *Good job*, I thought. He was subsequently banned from all McDonald's outlets within a 10-kilometre radius for two years. I milked that one, telling Josh his 'Wanted' photo was displayed at every McDonald's.

IF WE WERE THE OAKLEY Oval, the place all the kids gravitated towards when they were younger, we were promoted (?) to the place where older kids could crash after a big night out. Our house was conveniently within walking distance of town. Let's face it, it was better than drink–driving. No one could afford a taxi, and no one wanted to phone their parents for a lift at 3 a.m.

They didn't seem to realise their parents were probably lying awake anyway, waiting for the front door to open and bring that sense of relief they were home safe and sound.

We weren't keen on hosting parties on any grand scale. We'd had years of kids' birthday parties but not of the type Josh was suggesting. We eventually relented when Josh turned eighteen. We did all the right things: drew up a guest list, got permission from parents for their children to consume alcohol, sent a polite note to our neighbours, and organised a group of dads to be security guards. It was one of those occasions where you plan for the worst while hoping for the best.

Well, suffice to say it was an eye-opener. While we were ticking off invited guests at the door, other kids were scaling the fence around our property. Some arrived already inebriated and were asked to leave, and it seemed at one stage there were more people outside the property than in.

I was a pro at sniffing out contraband and scoured the house for bottles of alcohol, which they hid behind doors, in laundry hampers, under beds, in the garden. It was usually cheap but potent stuff.

The dads at the gate had their eyes out on stalks, but still, some of the shenanigans cannot be written about here. I had stern words with many revellers, including those jumping on the furniture — I just couldn't believe the disrespect for other people's property. Josh moaned that his friends thought I was psycho!

We survived the evening, and I did chuckle when one young girl turned up the next morning asking for her bottle of vodka.

Virtually every weekend boys would end up crashing at

our house after a night out. There were sometimes girls too, although they generally hid pretty well.

Despite trying to be quiet they *so* weren't. I would politely go downstairs in my dressing gown and ask them to keep it down. They would be sheepish and compliant. Ten minutes later I would go down again and let rip, telling them just to go to effing sleep. If there was a third occasion John would go down, and his response made mine look saintly. Ironically, in the morning John and I would creep around our own house so we didn't disturb them. Why *was* that?

We would give them till eleven o'clock, then I would cook them bacon and eggs and tell them it was time to bugger off. Secretly I loved hearing all the stories of the big night, and I loved the fact they were happy hanging out at our house. They can't have been too traumatised by the psychotic woman in her dressing gown because they would all turn up again the following weekend.

Our rules were simple: no drugs and no drink–driving.

When girls arrived in the mix it took some getting used to. Most who stayed the night left very early but certain girly items were often left behind, and their laughter and giggles were quite distinctive from the boys', so we knew. No one ever asked if their girlfriend could stay; it just happened.

The conversations were awkward. John didn't quite know how to broach the subject of sex and consent, and I wasn't much better. The boys would look at me as if to say, 'Yeah, yeah, yeah, hurry up — this is embarrassing.' While I am keen to be a grandmother, I didn't want it to be then.

Thankfully they managed to sort that out for themselves.

When we moved house I found a year's supply of condoms under the mattress of one of the beds. We figured that if they were in a relationship, it was better to be under our roof.

SIBLINGS ARE NOT NECESSARILY GOING to be best mates but I desperately wanted our boys to be close. It wasn't always the case but at Julian's thirtieth birthday recently I witnessed that special bond. They may not always like each other but I know they will always be there for each other.

On some occasions over the years, however, I have had serious concerns that they are really going to hurt each other.

A few years ago (2017) the boys were travelling to Auckland to play in the Cousins Shield, a hotly contested club squash event. It is the ultimate amateur teams event in New Zealand and the competition is part of our family history. My six brothers have played in the Cousins Shield, as has John. I have played in the female equivalent, the Mitchell Cup.

The boys loved the camaraderie, and constituted half the team. The Road to Cousins, as it came to be known, was the highlight of the squash calendar. John was the manager, and they represented the Devoy Squash Club so it was an extra-big deal for us.

The team was allowed one foreign import, so this year we had a young chap from Brisbane in the team. He had recently let one slip to the keeper, as my boys described it, and turned up to stay on the first night with his partner and very young baby. There wasn't much sleep that night as the little one howled his head off. In the morning John took the young family in his car, while the boys, wanting to distance themselves from the crying baby, took my car.

Alex, the oldest of our bunch going that year, drove. The customary stop on our trips to Auckland was the Copper Kettle, a pie and a toilet stop in Ngātea. My morning was interrupted by a text from Josh that was full of expletives, so I gathered something major had occurred. In short, Alex had driven off and left Josh at Ngātea. John had driven on, oblivious.

It transpired that Alex had told everyone to go to the toilet when they first arrived. Then when they were getting ready to leave, Josh announced that he was going to the loo. Outraged, Alex yelled: 'I told you to go before!' Then he revved the engine and took off, leaving Josh standing in the middle of the main drag.

He started walking the 100 kilometres home through the Karangahake Gorge. I got hold of John but he said he couldn't go back because he was already late for a managers' meeting at the North Shore Squash Club. I pleaded with Alex to go back.

He refused, and his parting words before he hung up were, 'Well, if you can't do the parenting then I will.' Ouch.

Eventually John had to go back and retrieve Josh. I knew there would be some tension, even some dire consequences, once the boys were in the same space. Unbelievably, they went on to win the event and all was forgiven and forgotten.

When each of the boys turned eighteen they enjoyed the right to do everything they had already been doing, but legally. They found great amusement in buying a beer wearing their school uniform and finally could go to the local nightclub without worrying about a false ID. The Bahama Hut, as it was known then, was the local hangout for all, but the drinks were expensive, especially if you had no income, so there was a bit of preloading at the Oakley Oval.

They seemed oblivious to the fact that their mother was lying awake all night listening for that comforting sound of the door opening. The sleepless nights returned.

TYPICALLY, KIWI KIDS LEAVE SCHOOL and get a job, an apprenticeship, or go to university. It definitely wasn't in our grand plan to end up with three sons at college in the United States.

Julian, the eldest, was a keen runner at high school — or at least he enjoyed the cross-country trips. A teacher said he thought Julian would be a good track runner, to which he replied, 'I don't really like running that much, sir.' But he gave it a crack and it turned out he was good, and he enjoyed it.

Eventually he applied for and received an offer of a full track and field sports scholarship from Providence College in Rhode Island. We were ecstatic — more than he was, in fact. He had a serious girlfriend by then and was not overly enthusiastic about leaving her behind.

But it was a no-brainer as far as we were concerned, and we were not going to take no for an answer. When the time came Julian and I spent a week or so staying with my brother Mark and his wife Julee in New York seeing the sights. It was my first time there and I loved it. But on the train to Rhode Island Julian sat there like a belligerent preschooler who didn't want to go to kindy. Not one word was spoken on that long train trip.

Even when we got there he stayed a few steps behind us, sulkily dragging his bags. I was beginning to think it really wasn't going to work. When we were introduced to the coach and assistant coach Julian perked up slightly, though he was clearly extremely nervous. Then a bouncy bubbly Kiwi girl whom Julian knew bounded up and took him off to show him around.

I arranged to meet him the next day at the mall to shop for any necessities. I immediately spotted him among a group of kids, their skinny bodies a giveaway that they were the middle-distance track team. Julian was as happy as Larry. I had booked myself into a hotel for a few days as a safety net, but I didn't see him again. All along we had encouraged him to just give it a go, and if he didn't like it he could come home. But he had to at least give it a crack. It was too good an opportunity.

I have no doubt it was hard, but he never complained about the volume of work or being homesick. He took to it like a duck to water and that was his life for the next six years, ending in a degree in finance and economics. Of course he came home for holidays, but he built a new life in the US. He was an all-American athlete.

Josh and Jamie had aspirations to follow their brother to college in the US. Alex chose to go to university in New Zealand — at Canterbury, then transferring to Waikato to study mechanical engineering. A young man of few words but very determined, he graduated with honours, as we found out on his graduation day. I never went to university myself — perhaps my one regret — and I am unashamedly proud that all my sons completed degrees.

All the boys were good squash players and Jamie and Josh were lucky enough to spend some time staying with Mark and Julee, who coached squash at Cornell University in New York. There was never any question of our boys scaling those lofty heights — Cornell is an Ivy League college and their academics didn't cut it.

They did, however, perform well enough at the US and Canadian Junior squash championships to catch the eye of some other university coaches. But being handy with a racket was the easy part. It was academic results that were the hurdle, particularly for Josh, who went to school to eat his lunch — if he went to school.

I had started at the Human Rights Commission when Josh was in his final year of high school and I often fielded calls or texts asking where Josh was. His attendance was slipping. Finally, I said to the deputy principal, 'Hey, you know where we live. How about you go around and ask him yourself?' I'd given up by then — there wasn't much more we could do.

Finally the penny dropped for Josh when he decided he wanted to go to college in the US and realised he had wasted the past couple of years. Suddenly he was determined to pass the SAT exam, the entry requirement for US colleges, so we hired a tutor to help him catch up.

We knew he was capable, but he was just one of those kids who would rather not try and fail, and preferred to live up to his reputation of the class joker. To his credit he passed his SAT, though his marks weren't going to get him into Harvard.

When he left I did have concerns about how he would cope with the workload, but in the end it was the making of him.

The worry didn't go away with Josh 14,000 kilometres away.

He joined the fraternity as a freshman, which isn't too common for first-years, but I think those Americans were enamoured with this mad Kiwi who was up for everything and obviously provided lots of entertainment. Josh had us in fits of laughter detailing the lengths he went to to get accepted into the fraternity.

Meanwhile Jamie had started at George Washington University in DC, where I hoped he would discover his real potential as a squash player and have an opportunity to have a crack at the professional circuit, but in reality that was my dream and not his, and I had to accept and respect that. He had a wonderful few years on the team and enjoyed his time at George Washington.

All of our sons' graduations were proud moments for John and me. We never insisted on them going to university but we were secretly delighted they did. I had never got a degree and John's diploma in meat technology didn't quite have the same ring to it as our boys' degrees. Each and every graduation was special in its own way; we were brimming with pride each time they walked across that stage. I jokingly tell people we haven't seen much of a return on our investment, but actually nothing could be further from the truth. They are fine young men (even if every mother says that about her sons!).

I am a little conflicted writing this. You will have noticed that Josh has used a lot of ink. He won't mind me writing about him — like his mum, he wears his heart on his sleeve. Despite many sleepless nights and lots of anxious moments for his mum, Josh has come out the other side, and, as Celia Lashlie promised me all those years ago, the boys are all okay. They are more than okay. Each and every one has his own personality — and a few of his mother's traits and a few of his father's. They are all forging their lives.

Parenting is the toughest job I have ever had, but also the most rewarding. I can't put into words just how much joy my sons have given me; raising them has certainly been my greatest achievement in life. I sometimes wonder what they would write about me as their mother if they were given the chance — let's not go there!

They don't need me as much now, and that's been a little hard to digest. It's weird. You bring them up to be independent, but when they finally are, you want to think they still need you.

As a mother you always want to be a mainstay in your child's life but you know that's absurd, especially as other women or partners enter their lives. I have no daughters to compare them with, but from observing friends with adult daughters I think I can confidently state that boys are a bit slacker about communication. They don't need or want their mother to know every detail about their lives — there is very little oversharing! In fact sometimes it's like getting blood out of a stone.

It's all gone so fast. That time with the newborn, the toddler, the teenager just flies by, and suddenly before you know it your 'children' are independent young adults forging their own lives.

I recall many years ago Pam Tremain, wife of All Black Kel Tremain, told me, 'Whatever you do, Susan, when they are older make sure you like their partners, because they will always choose them over you.'

I've been lucky in that respect. We have our first wedding

coming up soon in Boston in the US, when Lauren (affectionately known as Lulubelle) will officially join the clan. The boys' partners are a big part of our lives, and I'm lucky I don't have to pretend to like them. Lauren, Alice and Rachel are keepers and are now like daughters to me. I've found you can't help but become attached to the special others in your children's lives.

All my friends are becoming grandparents and John and I hope to join their ranks while we are still young enough. After Mum died in 2001 our boys only had one grandparent — John's mother, who lived in Christchurch and who they only got to see a few times a year. It would be lovely for their children to have more grandparents on hand.

But all I really want, deep down, is for my boys to be healthy and happy. That will be our job done.

Seven
Race Relations
Commissioner

I COULD WRITE an entire book on my term as race relations commissioner. 'The good, the bad and the ugly' would be an apt title.

I was bitter and twisted at the end of my term, due to various internal wranglings, but looking back I can see that on a whole lot of fronts it was a privilege to be in that role. There were amazing opportunities, real challenges and experiences that enriched my life. I hope my work achieved that for others as well.

It all began on a Sunday night in December 2012. I was folding mountains of washing and watching *Montana Sunday Theatre* when my cellphone rang. The caller introduced himself as Andrew Bridgman, CEO of the Ministry of Justice.

Instantly I thought, *Holy hell, either I or one of the kids must be in a power of trouble if the chief executive of the Ministry of Justice is ringing on a Sunday night*. He proceeded to tell me that Justice Minister Judith Collins had asked him to sound me out about applying for the role of race relations commissioner.

I was not unaccustomed to random requests, but this one stopped me in my tracks.

The conversation was short. I asked where the role was based, saying that I lived in Tauranga and didn't really want to move. John and I both later chortled at his response: 'It's not mission dependent.'

I gave him my email address and he said he would send me the job description and other relevant information and we would take it from there.

My mind was racing. This was certainly out of left field, but what an opportunity!

The email arrived the next day and the attached documents were full of the usual jargon and buzz words.

I looked at the application form and the large space to list qualifications, feeling a pang of my intermittent regret at never making the time to pursue a university degree. I didn't think a major in the university of life would cut the mustard.

Immediately I was filled with self-doubt. Then I looked at the role description and the applicant's personal attributes . . . I'm not sure if it's the case with all women, but we do tend to under-rate and undervalue ourselves, focusing on what we can't do as opposed to what we can. I fitted most of their criteria — there wasn't too much that threw me. Of course I would need to get up to speed with all the relevant legislation, but that was doable.

As you'll have realised by now, I live my life at full speed, and I'm sometimes impetuous. Strangely for an extrovert, I am also a pessimist. If that seems like a real contradiction, try living with it. I go guns blazing into things, full of confidence and energy, only to be stopped in my tracks by my own negativity. The mind is a powerful force, and it has been a lifelong mission to train myself to turn negativity and self-doubt into gratitude and optimism.

Sometimes you need to have someone in your life who can give you that positive affirmation, and I was lucky to have my friend Paula Thompson, my mentor in my Sport BOP days. I always went to her for wise counsel — she was always upfront and honest, telling me like it is.

Paula was as intrigued as I was by the offer, but her first response still rings in my ears: 'You know this is not a job for the faint-hearted.'

I said, 'Well, it's lucky I'm not faint-hearted!'

She more than anyone knows I sometimes leap into the unknown without due consideration, so she told me to make sure I did my homework. This would be a big step career wise and would have a huge impact on my family.

By this stage Julian was at college in the US, Alex was at the University of Canterbury, and Jamie and Josh were still at Tauranga Boys', Josh in his last year.

Opportunity had come knocking before but I had chosen to be around till the boys had finished school. This time something in the back of my mind was telling me that if I kept saying no, people might stop asking.

Another of my mother's sayings kept coming to mind:

'Susan, your children are your life but don't give up your life for them.' She was commenting on her own life to some extent. With a large family, she had no choices.

I made up my mind. I got my ducks in a row, completed all the relevant documentation, attached my CV and sent it down the line.

While the rest of New Zealand was still on holiday I was summoned to an interview in Wellington at the beginning of January 2013. Naturally I was nervous, especially when I saw some of the heavy hitters on the interview panel.

I thought I interviewed quite well; none of the questions stumped me. I sensed that some of them were not actually sure themselves exactly what the role entailed. One asked about my management style, but it turned out I would have absolutely no responsibility for staff.

I rang Paula after the interview and we chewed the fat. I had put my best foot forward and now I would have to wait.

And I waited and waited and waited — to the point where I virtually forgot about the job. I was hardly going to ring the minister to ask if she had made up her mind.

Six or seven weeks later I'd just hurled Jamie's cricket gear into the car and taken off when my phone rang. 'Hello, Dame Susan, it's Judith Collins here.' I hardly heard her because I was rushing — Jamie had forgotten his gear and I'd had to go back for it — so I said, 'Hey, look, I just have to get some gear to school for my son — got your number; I'll call you back.' And I hung up. Only then did it register. Oh — *that* Judith Collins. I swung into the carpark, composed myself and returned the call.

She offered me the position. It was a bolt from the blue and

I had a million questions, but my immediate response was yes. I played it cool, knowing there was plenty of administration to sort out before it was a done deal. We agreed I would divide my time between Auckland and Wellington. Our family circumstances were about to change, so John and I needed a chinwag, but he knew that once I had made up my mind about something there was no going back.

JUDITH COLLINS IS A FORMIDABLE woman. I travelled to Wellington to meet her for the first time. I am not a National Party patsy — in fact I have never been anyone's patsy. In her office I signed my warrant, which was effectively an employment contract, though slightly different.

She told me the race relations commissioner can do and say what they like, given that the role is independent of government, 'But I just ask that you tell me first.' The 'no surprises' message came through loud and clear and I immediately thought you would not want to cross her.

I am grateful to Judith; she was a good and fair minister, and well respected within the many different ethnic communities. Over time I worked under several ministers and prime ministers. The good ones, even if they didn't like being called out, knew I was just doing my job and they respected the office of the Human Rights Commission. Others paid lip service to human rights issues but did little about it.

Before I caught my flight home I was introduced to David Rutherford, the chief human rights commissioner. I was not able to enter the commission office on The Terrace until I had been officially welcomed with a pōwhiri, so I hung about awkwardly in the foyer, meeting a few staff who came to give me the once-over.

Then I hopped into a cab for the airport, feeling both nervous and excited. I switched on my phone and the thing just went off with a continuous chorus of pings of message alerts, missed calls and texts.

The news was out, before the official press release.

I listened to the first saved message and flicked through the texts. Immediately I saw that my appointment was proving controversial — already. Naively I had been imagining interview requests from media outlets and the odd congratulatory message, but I quickly realised that that was not the case.

I flew home not knowing what to think. As the car entered my street I noticed a posse of journalists congregating by my letterbox. Like a racing-car driver I put my foot on the gas and drove straight past. A blithering idiot, with no idea what to do, I drove up the driveway of a friend, an ex-policeman called Glen.

Rising to the challenge, Glen bundled me into the boot of his car like some underworld criminal. I am claustrophobic so it was terrifying, but it was the only way I was going to get home undetected. Desperate times called for desperate measures.

Glen got me safely home, then proceeded to berate the waiting journalists. Meanwhile Josh and his mates repeatedly drove up and down the driveway chanting 'She's not home', when in fact I had battened down the hatches inside and was wondering what the hell to do next.

Some media went into overdrive to dig up as much dirt on me as possible. They referenced old columns I had written, delved into my past and raked up as much muck as they could to back their theory that I was not qualified for the role.

My defence mechanism was to shut out all the noise. I could not control this maelstrom. I didn't listen to the news or read any newspapers, and stayed well clear of social media. This wasn't a new approach for me. Even before the invention of social media I had decided I couldn't control what journalists wrote about me so I wasn't going to read it.

I needed to show our boys I wasn't affected. As far as they were concerned, if Mum was okay then everything was okay . . . so I hid the stress, but I was actually a wreck inside.

A day or so later my senior advisor and the communications manager from the Human Rights Commission travelled to Tauranga to help plan a strategy. The media barrage felt like an orchestrated campaign designed to make me fail. I was attacked as a white woman, a sports jock, and labelled 'unsuitable for the role'.

My first few days at the office in Auckland I took the service lift to avoid the television crew camped out at the building's entrance. It was surreal. Never in my wildest dreams did I imagine it would be like this. I was getting a coffee one day and a complete stranger came up and said, 'Geez, you're getting a tough time. You'd think they would at least give you a chance to cock it up before they had a go at you.'

We went into damage control. I did a glossy spread for one of the women's magazines, smiling between gritted teeth, and the HRC communications manager suggested an interview with Michele Hewitson for a back-page spread in the *New Zealand Herald*. It would be 'semi-favourable', whatever that meant.

Meanwhile TV3 was pushing for me to appear on *Campbell Live*.

This was all new and foreign to me. I did the interview with Michele but it did not feel favourable. We sat in a café in Britomart and I felt powerless. I'd been under the pump so much it felt hard to believe anyone would write anything positive.

The next day the comms manager told me I was appearing on *Campbell Live*. I was so confused — for weeks he had been advising against it, so why the sudden change of heart? By this stage I didn't know whether I was Arthur or Martha and the advice kept changing. I have always admired John Campbell but also understood that he would have to do his job and I was going to be put through the ringer. I was coming close to breaking point.

I kept telling myself to be myself. The Campbell interview went well and no one could see my legs shaking uncontrollably under the table. John is fair, and I was able to answer his questions clearly and articulately.

That week the *Herald* article came out. It clearly was not favourable — in fact quite the opposite. I didn't even read it.

I drove back home after the Campbell interview feeling a small sense of accomplishment. It was late and the night was black. The last couple of weeks had been a nightmare but my gut instinct told me the interview was a watershed moment. I had to trust my gut. Surely things could not get any worse.

I know State Highway 27 like the back of my hand and on a long straight just before Paeroa I noticed these flickers of white light coming towards me. Before I knew it, I was just metres away from a herd of cows that had got loose. I slammed on the brakes and screeched to a halt in a ditch on the side of the road.

On the other side of the road was a small SUV with a cow splattered on the bonnet. It was mayhem and I was paralysed with shock — I couldn't even get out of the car.

Within minutes some farmers on tractors arrived and there were gunshots left, right and centre, with dead cows being dragged to the side of the road. The farmers were distraught.

In due course the emergency services arrived. A kindly policeman knocked on my car window to ask if I was okay. I thought I was so he said I could leave if I wanted, but my car kept revving and I couldn't get it out of the ditch. The officer had a go and instantly the car was back on the road. 'It helps if you put it in gear,' he said, smiling.

All the stress of the past few weeks suddenly combined with the night's lucky escape to overwhelm me and I collapsed into the policeman's arms. He drove me in my car to the Paeroa police station and after a cup of tea and a biscuit I tootled off home.

It's shameful to admit but I prayed for a major disaster or some other prominent person to fall foul, just to take the pressure off. They say today's news is tomorrow's fish-and-chip paper, but my story just kept on and on and I started to feel paranoid. The entire world probably wasn't watching my every move, but it certainly felt like it.

However, if I thought external forces were undermining me, I was about to face a whole raft of new challenges from inside the commission itself.

COMMISSIONERS HAVE COMPLEX ROLES: THEY are members of staff with an operational role as well as sitting on the governance board. So it was problematic knowing when to put on which hat. Also, there seemed to be no separation between governance and management.

Right from the outset there were internal tensions. The Human Rights Commission employs a chief human rights commissioner, a race relations commissioner, an equal employment opportunities commissioner, and a disability rights commissioner. A major restructure was under way when I started, which had dragged on for ages, and staff were anxious. Jobs were on the line and here I was coming in from the outside and making decisions about their futures. You know immediately when you walk into an organisation whether the culture is good or bad. This was not good.

The restructure was being sold as a new style of working, with lots of fancy corporate jargon surrounding the fact that we needed to cut costs, which meant getting rid of people.

It took me a while to get my feet under the table but I quickly came to understand that anything could happen — and often did.

There was a reactive component to my role, meaning that when a public figure (generally a politician) had a brain-fade and made a racist and/or derogatory comment, the media turned to me as some kind of adjudicator. Words hold immense power, particularly when spoken by those in influential positions, and it was my role to hold people to account when they crossed the line.

Winston Peters was a seasoned politician and in my opinion what made his remarks particularly unsettling was that they often seemed calculated, deliberately designed to convey a message to a specific audience. The term 'dog whistle politics' applies to a statement that might sound innocuous on the surface, but those attuned to this type of behaviour recognise the true intent.

Using race, especially as a tactic around election time, has become a favourite pastime for many politicians. Aspiring local MPs and councillors are always being invited to events, and given New Zealand's cultural diversity there is no shortage of events and festivals to attend. In an election year politicians of all stripes will flock to gatherings they would never normally attend, from the grand to the mundane, seizing the opportunity to connect with potential voters. They step up to the microphone, offer a few sound bites, take a selfie or two for their social media and then vanish. Over time you develop a keen sense for which politicians genuinely care about their constituents and which are merely chasing photo opportunities.

Winston Peters was a master at working the room, oozing charm and eloquence. I vividly recall an occasion at an Indian independence event just before the 2014 general election. Peters delivered a rousing speech about the Indian diaspora in our country, winning hearts and applause. Later that day he would make a comment that would reverberate far beyond that event. In discussing his intention to crack down on the sale of land to foreign buyers, something which had happened under both National and Labour governments, he said, 'Just because your predecessor did it too, does not make it sensible. As they say in Beijing, two Wongs don't make a white.'

The fallout was immediate and my office was inundated with complaints. Chinese New Zealanders let me know they were sick of being the brunt of insensitive jokes and ridicule. Amid the backlash one piece of anonymous mail stood out. Peters' face was superimposed on an image of a hospital patient with his leg in traction. The doctor was Asian, and the speech bubble said: 'Solly, wong leg.'

How do people not understand the insensitivity of the things they say?

I grew up reading *Little Black Sambo* and you don't have to be the race relations commissioner to know how inappropriate that is today. Times change, and it amazes me that people can't accept that we have evolved, and that it is positive to acknowledge change.

These types of incidents happened all the time. The woman in the gift shop selling 'golliwogs' just could not understand how they could be deemed offensive. She didn't understand the history of the term 'wog' and most definitely had never been called one.

I became immune to the personal criticism. It was easy to ignore the online comments as I didn't go anywhere near social media. But being bailed up in the supermarket or even by friends who thought I had gone over to the dark side was trying at times.

Often I would become the target of a campaign. My first experience was on a Saturday morning when I was walking up Mt Maunganui. My phone was in my pocket and started pinging every few seconds. I looked at the screen and saw a hundred or so emails in my inbox.

Each email was a picture of a white feather, awarded to me for cowardice. I was never sure exactly what prompted this, but circulating at the same time was a column written by someone who shall remain nameless but who obviously took great pleasure in including my email address at the end of their articles and suggesting people contact me directly. This became a regular occurrence.

Another time I came home to find my entire front door plastered with Hobson's Pledge leaflets. This right-wing lobby group led by Don Brash had a strong following in Tauranga — their rhetoric was anti-Māori and in particular anti-Treaty of Waitangi. Aside from being annoying they did not concern me too much and I came to expect their diatribes. If I commented in the media or wrote an opinion piece, they generally vehemently disagreed and this was their way of letting off steam.

I got a little more anxious when I received a threat to kneecap me, followed by a death threat. No one at the Human Rights Commission seemed too concerned. It was business as usual.

Every time the phone rang I got this uneasy feeling in my stomach and I soon recognised the phone numbers of most of the media outlets. They knew they were supposed to ring the office but always hoped to get past the gatekeepers. I wouldn't answer and immediately a text would follow with a request to comment.

As time went on I became accustomed to the hyperbole and attempts to make a story out of nothing, sensationalising something relatively minor.

GETTING AWAY FROM THE REACTIVE aspect of the job, as race relations commissioner I was patron of Auckland Regional Migrant Services, now called Belong Aotearoa. This organisation was set up to support refugee and migrant communities. There are a number of barriers to settlement for newcomers and the organisation is a welcoming and inclusive hub.

Many migrants are not Christians and do not celebrate Christmas, so one year the staff decided that they would remove all references to Christ in the promotion of their end-of-year luncheon to encourage everyone to come.

The headline in the *Herald* read: 'Multicultural seasonal advice: the word "Christmas" gets the heave-ho'. The journalist made the point that 'the agency has the backing of the Human Rights Commissioner, Tauranga's Susan Devoy'.

The public reaction was absurd. The way it was reported you would have thought I had the authority to abolish Christmas altogether.

There were moments like these when I struggled to understand how some people thought. Why did they take offence at something that had absolutely no impact on them personally? So-called Christians were taking umbrage at an organisation trying to include new New Zealanders with different beliefs and faiths in a Kiwi celebration.

Christmas cards are not so common these days but back then I was bombarded with cards to my office and home. I even had Christian tracts sent to me care of the local squash club. The messages of love and joy and the gift of Jesus were somehow buried under the vitriolic comments written in the cards.

I opened my back door early one morning to find a beautifully gift-wrapped Christmas present on my doorstep. When I opened it, it was full of dog faeces. It was not the parcel or its contents that disturbed me the most — it was the fact that someone had walked down our driveway in the middle of the night to leave it at the door.

I only had one physical confrontation. One morning I was walking up Mt Maunganui, my happy place and my regular exercise routine. John was with me and as we were descending from the summit a guy rushed at me and shoved me, yelling: 'You brown-loving bitch!' By the time I turned around he had disappeared around the corner.

John and I were stunned, and kept walking, trying to digest what had happened. By the time we got to the bottom I was *angry*, and I took it out on poor John. 'Did you not see what happened?' I said to him. 'If someone had abused you, I would have chased them and smashed their lights out.' Nothing like this had ever happened to either of us before and it had just come so out of the blue.

Ninety per cent of the complaints to my office had a similar theme — they were anti-Māori and anti-Treaty, from angry Pākehā, predominantly male. These people were so threatened, so scared and so angry about losing something that wasn't theirs in the first place. I always replied politely, however tempted I was at times to tell them where to go. It gave me great satisfaction to type a minuscule *fu* at the end of an email.

I can't resist including a sample — there were hundreds more. These were received after we launched a campaign called That's Us, in which we asked people to share their experiences:

With one in four people in NZ not being born here, the cultural identity that drew these immigrants here in the first place is under threat.

THAT causes racism. So why not nip it in the bud with a more balanced immigration system? Immigration without assimilation is invasion.

Simply turning parts of the country into districts of India or China does not assimilate people. It merely resettles them like (koi) carp. To add insult to injury I have had migrants tell me that NZ doesn't even have a culture. We are just English. Like a Canada or an Australia.

Race relations could also be improved by immigrants showing some gratitude and fucking respect. But why would they when everything alien is celebrated here and any white person who shows pride in their history is called a racist?

Because the answer to what 'kind of country we want our kids growing up in' is FUCKING NEW ZEALAND. It is disappearing. That is resented.

Do generations of young Māori terrorising communities count as 'racism, intolerance and hatred'?

There are enough very real issues in this country without you inventing new grasping reasons to claim victimhood.

It was hard at times to remain upbeat and not be overwhelmed by all the negativity. Initially I thought this was a reflection of the fact that I was doing a terrible job, but I quickly came to see that it probably meant the opposite.

Every now and then people did send in considered, well-thought-out views and opinions that proved valuable in helping shape the narrative. Dare I say it, I even received the occasional compliment.

THE POSITIVE SIDE OF MY role was the interaction with the many and varied multicultural groups I met. Attending their events and functions I was anxious at first — I was new, and keen to make a good impression.

I knew I had to earn their respect and, more importantly, their trust. And this was where I found the joy of my role. There was no shortage of cultural events and celebrations to attend and they opened up whole new worlds to me. New Zealand is home to people from all over the globe. I would rock up and be treated like a VIP.

Diwali, Chinese New Year, Ramadan and Eid are becoming more mainstream in New Zealand and offer opportunities for all Kiwis to participate in rich experiences to help them understand how these events are significant for their culture.

I am a people person, so after the formalities were over I would often stay and chat with the organisers and some guests. I have never eaten so many delicious curries and dumplings in my life but the highlight was the relationships I fostered, which were critical to my success in the role.

I looked forward each year to Race Relations Day, when all around the country different towns and cities would host events. During my time we expanded the celebrations to include multicultural festivals, sporting events, speech competitions and food festivals, and even had the privilege of hosting two major events at Government House in Auckland.

One Race Relations Day at Government House was spectacular, spoiled only by an 'off' comment by a staff member in yet another reminder that we still have a long way to go. It was a beautiful sunny day and the garden was full of people from all different cultures celebrating together. As we were clearing up and getting ready to go, one group were still congregating on the lawn when a senior member of the governor-general's staff came up to me. She had had a face like a twisted sandshoe all day, sighing and rolling her eyes.

She pointed to a group of Ethiopian women who had been making their customary coffee for the guests and asked me to tell 'those people' to leave. I rolled my eyes at her.

I met some fabulous human beings and forged friendships for life, which was undoubtedly the unexpected bonus of my job. I would never have met so many people from so many different ethnicities and walks of life, had I not been the race relations commissioner.

There was one gentleman I saw at virtually every event — he was hard to miss in his smart police officer's uniform. He was always on hand to escort me to my seat, and introduce me to the event organisers or other people who I needed to know. He was like a guardian angel sent to guide me.

Superintendent Rakesh Naidoo had become the police's first

Asian liaison officer in 2004. We quickly became friends and allies. He knew the issues, and working together we used both our positions to do some really good mahi. So good in fact that I managed to convince Rakesh to take a secondment from the police and become my principal advisor for nearly three years.

He looked very dapper on his first day at the commission, given that I had never seen him out of uniform. He lived and breathed his job and by all accounts still does. Sometimes I used to wonder if he ever slept. There was no one and nothing he didn't know within New Zealand's ethnic communities.

Our common ground was that we both had the interest of our communities at heart, and neither of us was afraid to tackle issues head on. The New Zealand Police do some amazing community policing that largely goes under the radar. I quickly gained respect for all the ethnic police liaison officers I met.

If Rakesh was a star, I met another gem in Jessica Phuang, currently the police ethnic responsiveness manager for Auckland. She was everybody's aunty. She took a real interest in supporting young migrants, particularly international students. Jessica gathered around her a senior group often referred to as aunties and uncles, predominantly Asian and all with a real heart for issues in the local community. She ran courses and seminars; participants were her ears and eyes on the streets, and she was their link back to police to ensure their communities were safe and were heard.

Before Covid-19 put paid to international student numbers, education was a billion-dollar business for New Zealand and the students at some institutions were treated a bit like cash cows. Both Jessica and Rakesh brought a number of serious incidents to the attention of our office.

Asian students had been reported as being the victims of assaults and robberies, and when we organised a meeting at Auckland University for students and concerned stakeholders we came to understand that this was the tip of the iceberg. Once we started delving we exposed a whole raft of systemic failures. I will always remember Naisi Chen, president of the Chinese Students' Association, an articulate and impressive woman who was one of Labour's youngest MPs in 2020–23. Naisi was instrumental in galvanising the students and getting them to attend the meeting we had organised. They were able to tell us first-hand about their experiences.

People in government agencies and educational institutions needed to understand that international students were not just an economic commodity, they were actual human beings, and if we had welcomed them into our country then we needed to look after them.

It's always trying to get officials to take an issue seriously, but where serious harm is being done, getting someone to do something about it should never be as difficult as it is. Our office wanted to have a code of conduct and some guidelines for pastoral care included in the new international well-being strategy. Seriously, how hard could that be?

There were endless meetings with the various government agencies and progress was at a snail's pace. At times the action list did not seem to include any action at all. The inertia drove me crazy as meetings went round and round in circles.

In one meeting I suggested that I could use the statutory powers of the Human Rights Commission to launch an inquiry.

Left My favourite photo of me as a baby (there are only two). Mum and I were never known for conforming, so there's some irony in us reading *The Ten Commandments* together.

Right My six bros — all rocking 1980s moustaches — celebrating my twenty-first birthday with me.

Right Posing with the trophy after winning the British Open in 1985. *Photographer unknown; used with permission of the New Zealand Squash Hall of Fame*

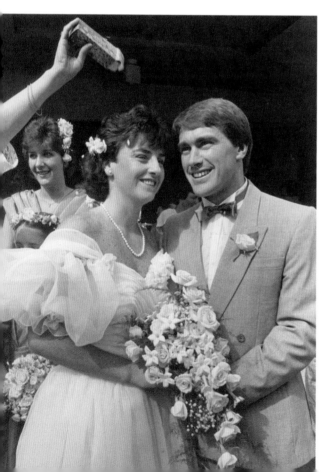

Left It was a big day! Our wedding in my hometown of Rotorua on 13 December 1986. We're still going strong more than 35 years later. *Rotorua Post*

Left On court at the New Zealand Squash Open with Liz Irving, one of the nicest players on the circuit. *Stuff Limited*

Right One of my favourites: winning the 1987 World Championships on home soil in Auckland. *Frances Oliver*

Top The apple of my father's eye! I wish Dad had lived long enough to see all his grandsons; he would have loved them.

Above John has been my rock and we have shared some magical moments.

Top The photo that appeared on the front page of the *New Zealand Herald* when I was announced as a recipient in the Queen's Birthday Honours in 1998. I never imagined being a Dame!

Above It was always a busy household with my four boys around. I'm so grateful they have grown up to be good mates. From left: Jamie, Julian, Josh and Alex.

Left Always the life and soul of the party: my amazing mother, Tui.

Right Attending an event with then Prime Minister Jacinda Ardern and Labour MP Priyanca Radhakrishnan during my time as Race Relations Commissioner. I admired our PM for wearing traditional dress, but I was always too self-conscious to do so myself.

Top Cartoonist Tom Scott's take on the work I was doing as Race Relations Commissioner to call for an inquiry into historical abuse in state care. I don't consider myself in the same league as Dame Whina Cooper, but to have played a part in the inquiry with the team at the Human Rights Commission was a humbling and rewarding experience. *Alexander Turnbull Library, DCDL-0035976; used with permission of Tom Scott*

Above All the family together for Josh's graduation in the US in 2019. I couldn't be prouder of all my sons. They're fine young men, so that's a job well done.

Above *Celebrity Treasure Island* came out of the blue but it was a hell of a ride! *WBITVP NZ*

Right Me and my rock.

Bingo! That got a reaction, as I discovered later in the day. I was walking to Parliament for a function. It was a cold dark night and everyone was disguised under big winter coats. The women behind me were chatting about their day when one said to the other, 'Dame Susan was at a meeting today about international students. What would she know about education?' I turned around and said, 'Apologies for eavesdropping but I am Dame Susan.' You should have seen her jaw drop. She introduced herself as a senior executive with the Ministry of Education. I knew exactly who she was and I also knew she hadn't attended the meeting. We exchanged a few polite words and went on our merry way.

Moments later I received a text. I now suddenly had a meeting with the CEO of the Ministry of Education in the morning and the minister in the afternoon. That was fast. I came to understand that ministers don't like inquiries almost as much as they don't like surprises.

Part of the role of the Human Rights Commission is to hold the government to account, but that's often easier said than done. The role of each and every commissioner is to speak truth to power. To stand up for what's right, no matter who the 'offender' is. It's never comfortable confronting authority but people are relying on you to do so. You are their voice, and you need to be heard.

I certainly didn't relish sitting in the office of a minister or a senior public servant remonstrating with them, but it was part of my job because most people are scared to speak up and call out any sort of injustice. The fear of reprisal, of losing your job, of being shunned by colleagues is second only to the fear that you won't be believed. The power imbalance is often huge.

It is a bit like saying my door is always open, but only if you tell me what I want to hear.

Speaking up is tough, and the most difficult time to speak up is when you are afraid. God, there were times when I was so afraid of saying what needed to be said that my voice would quiver, but you don't have the luxury of waiting until the fear subsides before you say something or the moment is lost.

I had to keep reminding myself to speak without apology because people without a voice were relying on me. Senior officials would look at me with disdain as if to say, 'What would you know about it?'

At the risk of incurring the wrath of male readers, I have to say it is harder for women. Irrespective of their political leanings, no one could seriously deny that the attacks on Jacinda Ardern when she was prime minister were more vitriolic than they would have been if she was a man.

THERE WERE TIMES IN MY role when I experienced sorrow and joy simultaneously, and there were many occasions and events that had a profound and lasting effect on me personally. They still upset me but I no longer have the platform to effect change.

In any job there are parts you enjoy more than others. I particularly loved working with refugee organisations and meeting some of the refugees who come to New Zealand. Many Kiwis have a narrow view and are reluctant to see the country take more refugees, but this attitude is born out of ignorance and even fear. We are a relatively wealthy, peaceful country and have a responsibility to assist the desperate.

We have been doing it for years. It was 80 years ago when Prime Minister Peter Fraser welcomed more than 700 Polish child refugees from war-torn Europe when no one else would help. They had survived the Nazis, endured life in Soviet work camps and trekked from Siberia to Iran before they boarded a troop carrier that brought them across the world to Wellington. New Zealanders watched these emaciated youngsters, most of them orphans, walking silently down the gangway, and the Kiwis gathered said they had not been prepared for the raw emotion and empathy they felt for these tiny children.

Helen Clark did something similar in 2001 when she welcomed 150 asylum seekers Australia refused to accept, commonly referred to as the *Tampa* refugees.

I would become emotional each time I visited the Māngere Refugee Resettlement Centre. It doesn't matter where they have come from — Syria, Afghanistan, Myanmar, South America — they have all fled horrors we can only imagine. Coming to New Zealand for them was not a lifestyle choice, it was a matter of survival.

Who could not be touched by the children singing our national anthem in te reo Māori and seeing the gratitude on their parents' faces for finally being safe? I often wished everyday New Zealanders had the opportunity to witness some of these occasions so they would feel more compassion.

Yes, I understand that we have a chronic housing shortage that has compounded our homelessness problem. We have too many children living in poverty, but it shouldn't be a 'them or us' situation. As an international citizen New Zealand has a responsibility to play a part. As a country we like to think we punch above our weight, but when it comes to our refugee quota we are failing miserably.

When refugees have completed their six-week induction programme at Māngere there is a beautiful farewell as they embark on their next journey in their new country. These were special occasions and I owe a great deal to Sonny Bill Williams, who often came along. Most of the newcomers had not heard of him, having come from countries where football was the national sport, but word quickly went around that he was an All Black, and everyone has heard of them.

It was the fact that he was Muslim that endeared him to people. He was someone like them — he would be bombarded by excited kids and their families. Sport is a wonderful ice-breaker: throw a ball into any situation and immediately there is a bonding factor. SBW was gracious and generous and made an enormous impact.

The Human Rights Commission was just a small part of the campaign to increase the refugee quota. We seldom worked in a silo — there are many organisations (mostly run on the smell of an oily rag) advocating for others under the human rights umbrella.

WE RAN EFFECTIVE CAMPAIGNS, AT all times conscious of our limited resources and the scrutiny of our use of taxpayer money. One was simply titled Never Again. Some time into my term I became aware of the report of the Royal Commission into Historical Abuse in State Care, led by former chief commissioner Rosslyn Noonan. The report had been completed in 2011 but was never published.

Noonan left the commission and the report to her successor. The new chief commissioner, David Rutherford, told investigative reporter Aaron Smale that he and a team of lawyers found the report's conclusions were legally flawed, which is why it was not published.

I knew nothing of this until later in my term, after reading Smale's reporting for Radio New Zealand. Suddenly the report was back on the table.

The stated reason for not publishing the report initially was that it contained numerous inaccuracies. What was not inaccurate was that an enormous amount of abuse had taken place and by all accounts was still happening. It seems to me the government always challenges reports that call into question its own involvement. They know it shines a spotlight, and might end up costing them money. But this report highlighted atrocities that are a scourge on our society.

The commission called on survivors of historical abuse to send us stories and photographs and we had an unprecedented response. Hundreds of heart-breaking stories poured into our office. I read versions of the same story over and over. A young boy back in the day was caught stealing lollies from a Four Square store. A report labelled him a thug and he was made a state ward at ten years old. In a boys' home he was physically and sexually abused and ended up doing long stretches in isolation — months at a time alone in a single cell. He was still a child. While he was there his parents died.

When he was let out he was sent to live with a series of

families, some of whom also abused him both physically and sexually. He went on to spend time in and out of prison. He was an old man by the time he made meaningful contact with his family again and by then he'd lost just about everything — language, whakapapa, whānau, and childhood.

This was the tragic story, with minor variations, we heard from thousands of men and women. Many were not Māori, but New Zealand children were more likely to be put in state institutions if they were. This is the very definition of institutional racism — the systemic discrimination and unconscious bias that many would have you believe doesn't exist. Many people have been calling it out for years.

Soon after we launched an open letter calling on New Zealanders to back our call for a public inquiry, the phones started ringing. Former institution staff telling us they were instructed to take only Māori children; a former police officer who confirmed that children were picked up for little or no reason, and he had never thought twice about the fact that every child he dropped off at a children's home was Māori. He felt sick with guilt on realising the suffering they had endured.

More than 100,000 children and vulnerable adults were taken in by the state between the 1960s and 1990s and we knew many were subjected to abuse. A public inquiry was essential to determine the nature and extent of the abuse, and to support changes in our current welfare system. The fact that previous governments had refused was nothing short of abhorrent.

In the 1950s and 60s over 80 per cent of the youngsters held in state welfare homes were Māori. Decades later, more than half our prison population is Māori. That is not a coincidence.

Social justice advocates, academics and survivors themselves tell us those homes were little more than a pipeline to prison. Our office became convinced that the removal of Māori children into welfare institutions by the state was the start of systemic and mass imprisonment of Māori New Zealanders.

In August 2017 I was at the United Nations Office in Geneva. Every five years the government reports to CERD, the international Committee on the Elimination of Racial Discrimination, on how we are tracking. The HRC also prepares a report recommending areas for improvement. It's a bit like a game of ping-pong: we challenge the government and they respond, but on a world stage. This year we called on the New Zealand government to initiate an independent inquiry into state abuse, and that call came through as a strong recommendation by the UN when the CERD report was released.

It was a watershed moment when Labour won the 2017 election, and an inquiry into state care was one of the first announcements made by the incoming prime minister, Jacinda Ardern. I am proud of my part in that, and years later I still marvel at the courage of all those survivors. It's not over yet for them, but relentlessly they continue to tell their stories, and I understand the pain it causes them each and every time. They're not doing it for themselves.

Generations of Māori have experienced racism and prejudice. Quite aside from the numerous Treaty of Waitangi breaches, Māori New Zealanders have faced not just casual discrimination but legislated discrimination. Old-age pensions and widows' benefits were initially lower for Māori. Māori war veterans after World War Two received fewer benefits and opportunities than other returned servicepeople. When they arrived home they were still banned from entering licensed premises. How many New Zealanders today know that Māori Battalion vets were not welcome in many hotels, bars and restaurants on their return from war? Racism is generally not so overt these days, but it still exists.

A third of the complaints to the commission in my day were to do with racism, but we knew that most people when they were refused a flat or humiliated in front of their class or workmates never formally complained. So this was our initial challenge: to encourage everyday New Zealanders to raise their voices and share their stories of racism, to counter the views of some Kiwis who simply don't believe racism exists in Aotearoa.

In September 2016 we launched New Zealand's first nation-wide anti-racism campaign, That's Us, calling on New Zealanders to talk about the prejudice they've faced growing up in this country. MPs, mechanics, award-winning scholars, aged-care workers, cleaners: they all shared stories about the prejudice that exists in those quiet places.

There was the teacher who told you God didn't love the Tūhoe people because they were terrorists; your classmates who joked that your family car was stolen; the man who assumed you were the cleaner when you were actually a university lecturer; the supermarket staff who racially profiled you. Some people like to call these instances 'casual racism', but it certainly doesn't feel casual when you or your family are humiliated or denied opportunities. And it affects everyone from university students to chief executives to cooks to millionaires.

The young man in the Tūhoe story told us:

Over the years I'd get used to having to defend everything Māori. During class discussions other kids would argue that the Treaty is racist or that Māori scholarships are racist. Once I got up to say that my scholarship came from my tribe, not from the government, and someone shouted out 'Hone Harawira!' from the back of the class and everyone laughed at me. The teacher did nothing. Being a Māori kid in a mostly Pākehā world — yeah. You're often put on the spot whether you like it or not. One minute you're defending your tribe in class. Next minute you get told to lead the haka or speak at a pōwhiri for the school.

A senior executive told us: 'I recall as a young university lecturer working late in my office one night and being asked by security if I was the cleaner; as a freshly minted CEO attending a CEO forum being asked if I was "in the right place"; and at the council office paying my rates being asked if this house was really mine.'

People shared their personal stories, and the response was immediate and profound. These heartfelt, real stories had more than three million website hits.

Some of the bravest Kiwis I've ever met are our Jewish Holocaust survivors. Inge Woolf, founder of the Holocaust Centre, told me once that hate starts small. It started in Nazi Germany with kids at school — and some teachers — making fun of or humiliating Jewish children. Hate grew with ads in the paper that said Jews weren't allowed to do this or that. Pretty soon Jews weren't allowed to do anything, and started being rounded up and taken away.

But this kuia also said hope starts small. Hope starts when people stand up for what is right. Hope grows when a bystander sticks up for a stranger who is being abused. When a workmate refuses to laugh at the racist joke.

Racism starts small and is a light feeder. If we feed it, racism grows and turns into racial hatred. This is what we are seeing in some places overseas and it's what we never, ever want to see here in Aotearoa.

We called the next leg of our campaign (in 2017) Give Nothing to Racism, because we needed to remind Kiwis that racism feeds off our thoughts, prejudices and actions. All racism needs to grow is us, so we need to give it nothing. When we laugh off little pieces of racism because we don't like tension, when we try to excuse them, defuse them, what we're doing is passively agreeing with the racist.

What if we didn't? What if we frowned instead of laughed? What if we blanked our mates instead of nodding? What if, instead of walking past, we asked the woman in a head-scarf who was being abused if she was okay?

This is what we asked of New Zealanders.

I lost count of the number of times a mum or dad asked me what their child should do when they faced racist taunts on the way home from school. I sometimes wondered whether they themselves were people who sometimes stood by, ignoring what was going on in front of them.

As Kiwis we all need to check ourselves and our own behaviour. But we need to do it in a Kiwi way — a way that can reach young people. A way that reminds us that racism is not something we like to think Kiwis practise. So we asked the famous, funny and beloved Taika Waititi, 2017 New Zealander of the Year, to make an anti-racism video.

The video Taika helped us put together was classic Kiwi comedy — satirical, funny, hard case, hard-hitting. Next, we approached some of Aotearoa's most beloved actors, musicians, athletes, comedians, journalists and leaders to get involved. Kieran Read, Moana Maniapoto, Sam Neill, Miriama Kamo, Sir Graham Henry, Karen Walker, Witi Ihimaera, Hayley Holt, Sonny Bill Williams, Tim Finn, Tana Umaga, Wetini Mitai-Ngatai, Lucy Lawless, Sir John Kirwan, Tiki Taane, Holly Walker, Ru Perera, Oscar Kightley . . . the list goes on. They all came in and recorded video memes of them Giving Nothing to Racism.

Their memes sparked hundreds of people to record their own videos, and before long we had schools and companies joining in. Our anti-racism campaign that year reached almost eight million people. Our videos were viewed and our stories read and shared by millions.

We can stop 'casual racism' from growing into something more extreme. We can give it no encouragement. No respect. No place. No power. We can give nothing to racism. This highly effective campaign was developed by the dedicated and committed staff at the Human Rights Commission, a small tight team with limited resources who really believed in our mahi.

I LEFT THE COMMISSION IN 2018 when my five-year term ended. If the beginning of my term had been difficult, the end was no better — for different reasons.

At the time the commission was hampered by a lot of internal dysfunction. It had also just undergone a major restructuring. Right from the outset I observed behaviour that I felt was unacceptable, in a culture of victimisation, sexual harassment and bullying. Some of the things I witnessed would have been unacceptable in any organisation but the Human Rights Commission should have been leading by example.

I had spoken out about a number of things, but it all came to a head over the manner in which the HRC handled a serious internal sexual harassment complaint. For me, this really was the straw that broke the camel's back. I called it out, as is my style, but despite my best efforts nothing substantial seemed to change. It may have just been my perception, but I often felt like a lone wolf.

Eventually, in 2017, Justice Minister Andrew Little instituted a ministerial review into the institutional culture of the organisation, led by retired judge Coral Shaw. Judge Shaw's report in May 2018 cited 'a deep divide between some staff and some managers' and 'uncooperative and unprofessional dynamics' between commissioners. The report also cited 'a chronic lack of the resources required for the Commissioners to undertake the work of the HRC, caused by the Government's long-term cap on funding'. There were several recommendations for positive change.

I could have handled things differently, but given my time again I probably wouldn't. I have always done things for the right reasons but perhaps not the right way, and I concede that my style seems to keep getting me into hot water. But I can lie straight in bed at night knowing I did what I did in the best interest of others, with no self-interest at play.

I didn't buckle under pressure to conform even when as commissioners we were told that if we were not united, we would have our warrants taken off us, which in my opinion felt like a veiled threat that we would be fired.

What I learnt is that being a whistle-blower is tough, and sometimes the very processes designed to uncover the truth end up protecting the guilty. Standing up and speaking out often comes at great personal cost. If you rock the boat, you get wet!

It will be a time in my life that I will never forget.

Eight
Empty-nesters

NOT LONG AFTER I started as race relations commissioner in 2013 John was offered a transfer to Melbourne. He worked for Lima Orthopaedics, a large international company, and had been the general manager of the New Zealand business for nearly fifteen years. He loved the job, and was flattered to be asked. The expectation was he would manage both countries during his tenure, so it would be a massive workload, but John has never been afraid of hard work.

Needless to say, the timing couldn't have been worse. I was now in a very busy job: how would we make this work? We were already like ships in the night, going for days without seeing each other, occasionally catching up if we happened to be in the same city.

Josh was working and studying for the SAT entrance exam for college in the US, and Jamie was still at school (somewhat reluctantly, I might add). Were they aware of their parents working their bollocks off to pay for it all? Who knows.

Anyway, John negotiated a deal whereby he would commute, spending two weeks running the New Zealand office (from Auckland and Tauranga), then two weeks in Melbourne.

Looking back, I don't know how we did it. At times it was a logistical nightmare, but after 40 years of being together I can see that perhaps that was the secret to our success: spending some time apart. The nature of our work and the fact that we lived in Tauranga meant commuting became the norm. There was no danger of us ever being stuck in a rut . . .

It's always been an unspoken rule that we each allow the other the freedom to do what they want — within reason of course. It wasn't selfish: everything we did was for our family and the end game, but we each had a strong drive to be individually successful in our chosen careers. Some might say it looked like I wore the pants in the family, but only when he agreed I should put them on. It's worked for four decades. When at times it got tough, John would always say, 'It is what it is.' And we'd get through.

Gradually the periods John spent in Australia got longer and longer and soon we were lucky if he got home once a month. The bonus was that he lived in a very cool apartment in Port Melbourne, so the boys and I never needed a reason to go and visit.

WHEN JOSH WENT OFF ON a squash scholarship to college in upstate New York, Jamie was the only one left. He was having a stellar year on the squash court and was selected for the New Zealand Junior Men's team to compete in the world championships in Poland. He told us he didn't want to complete year 13 at school and also wanted to apply for a squash scholarship to the US.

These college applications are no walk in the park and involve a lot of paperwork. 'Admin' became a much-used word in our household. So as well as working, John spent hours sifting through all this. Luckily, he is a 'details' sort of guy — the boys had no idea how much work it took. When Jamie was accepted on the squash team of George Washington College in Washington DC in 2016, we became empty-nesters.

John's deal with his employer was that when the last of our boys had left home he would live permanently in Melbourne, so it was just me left at home in Tauranga. Our once bustling, noisy family home that held so many fabulous memories was suddenly deathly quiet. The house needed a lot of work — over the years we had thrashed it. Neither John nor I are very good at (or even interested in) DIY stuff, not to mention not having the time, so we just kept putting off a decision about what to do with the house.

Then one day out of the blue a real estate agent approached us with an offer. John happened to be back from Melbourne for a few days and it seemed as if the stars were aligned. We sold and bought within a week — and we didn't have to do the DIY.

We had often thought about moving to Mt Maunganui and this deal forced our hand. Driving over to look at a house we had a few cross words — I can't remember what about, but I know I was fuming. I walked into the house and had a quick look around. I sat on the couch, which had a beautiful view of Mt Maunganui, and said, 'This will do.' It was exactly what we needed — a 'lock and leave' that suited our current lifestyle. Besides, we didn't have time to faff around or I'd be homeless.

A downside to us both working so hard and being separated for long periods was that when we were together, neither of us wanted to burden the other with the woes of our stressful lives. We didn't want the little time we had together to be a whinge fest. Well, to tell the truth, when it comes to whingeing I would always win hands down. Sometimes his eternal optimism wore me down and I would let him have it.

My problem was that my work put me under enormous public scrutiny. If I had a bad day I could read about it the next day on the front page, and keyboard warriors were always taking potshots. Then I would come home to an empty house and have no one to offload on. It was tough. I think we both knew this arrangement couldn't last forever, but in the meantime we just boxed on through the tough times.

John loved coming home and I loved visiting him in Melbourne. For me, Melbourne was the ultimate escape — a cool, vibrant city where I loved being completely anonymous. There was always something sporty to go to and plenty else to see and do. When John came to the Mount he enjoyed the new pad and getting away from the pressure of his job.

The last few months of my term at the Human Rights Commission were torrid and I couldn't wait to get on a plane and get the hell out of New Zealand. I had been putting on a brave face, but the truth is that I was spent, physically and emotionally.

Generally I can shake myself out of any malaise by getting out and walking, but it wasn't working. I would drag my sorry arse around the Mount, where normally I would be up and down like a mountain goat. I was still functioning but had no energy and zero enthusiasm. I would come home exhausted and unable to do anything but drink a couple of glasses of wine. I knew this wasn't helping but I couldn't have cared less. Then I would go to sleep. It's a sad state of affairs when the highlight of your day is going to bed.

Quite by chance someone I knew said to me after coffee one morning, 'You're not good, are you, Susan?' She obviously saw the signs. I knew she had fought and conquered her own demons, and her intervention was the catalyst I needed to seek help. My first appointment with the doctor was tough. I knew something wasn't right but it was so hard trying to articulate it.

To this day only John knows how bad I got. The doctor prescribed medication for anxiety and depression and this made me feel like an abject failure. I was tough and staunch: couldn't I work my way out of this slump without pills? But the reality was that the stress of the last few years — and particularly the manner in which my term at the HRC had ended — had taken its toll. I was so strung out that this manifested itself in some serious panic attacks. I didn't want to take any prescribed medication but finally relented. When I did, I assumed the medication would be an instant fix but it wasn't, and that made me feel worse. I stuck at it, but it wasn't helping.

I found it really hard to open up and explain how I felt. The biggest challenge was trying to get it across to John, across the ditch in Melbourne. Once again, our different personalities came to the fore: the optimist versus the pessimist. No matter how bad things got, John would always count his blessings. Sometimes it drove me to distraction but the truth is I am envious of his ability to keep looking forward and feel gratitude for what he has. John loves to have a plan — he thinks anything can be solved by making a list. Quite often I wanted to shove those lists up his . . .

I knew he was only trying to do his best for me but the more helpful he was, the shittier I got. It's true that you take things out on those closest to you. I couldn't — or didn't — share this with anyone else, so he wore it all.

I did find the courage to have some counselling, and in the first few sessions I just let it all out. It was cathartic — there was a lot to unravel. I had never imagined something like this would happen to me. When I look back I can see there were signs; I just didn't recognise or acknowledge them. It had all been building for a while and suddenly hit me like a ton of bricks.

I felt like a zombie, down about everything, but the scary part was I had also become super anxious about virtually everything. My first anxiety attack was on an aeroplane. On a hot and humid day the plane landed at Auckland Airport. It taxied for a little bit, then came to a halt. People were standing up getting their bags when the captain came over the PA and said we had to wait for the gate to become free, so would people please remain seated. Some people kept right on fossicking for their bags and instantly my temperature rose. It felt like a menopausal hot flush on steroids as I stood up and yelled at everyone to sit down. They did.

I was so hot. I peeled off as many clothes as I could but it didn't help. Then I started hyperventilating. I had never experienced anything like it before — it was so scary. But I'm generally not good with confined spaces so I put it down to claustrophobia and menopause. Then suddenly I realised I was having a panic attack. And it wasn't the last — it was the start of a difficult few months. The counselling was a life-saver, as was getting back into my regular exercise regime and being kinder to myself.

MY SALVATION WAS MOVING TO Melbourne, almost a year after I finished at the HRC.

I enjoyed the early days living in a new city but it took some adjustment for John and me to live together again 24/7. In the weekends we were like newlyweds. There were no distractions, it was just us and we got out and explored Melbourne. It wasn't just the city; we indulged our love of hiking and tramping and took the odd bike ride. I should add here that these are all much more John's passions than mine. It's like being married to the Energizer Bunny.

John had joined a Melbourne bush walkers club and looked forward to his Sunday tramps. I wasn't so enamoured but went along for the ride — generally a long bus ride to a destination very similar to the previous week's. The Australian bush is not quite the same as New Zealand's; instead of lush green native bush it was miles of dry, brown, dusty gum trees — with snakes. I took heed of the warnings: the first tramper wakes the snake, the second jumps over it, and the third gets bitten. And these brown snakes are deadly.

We encountered one once. John had suggested a walk to a popular tourist spot, adamant that we wouldn't see snakes because there were too many people about. *Since when have snakes been scared of tourists?* I wondered. He was striding ahead of me and I saw the long brown shape slither in front of him. He had all his fingers and toes crossed that I hadn't seen it as it disappeared into the distance.

Walking in Australia never lived up to the beauty of tramping in New Zealand, and John was a little worried I might say so to his Aussie walking buddies, but I managed to bite my tongue when they oohed and aahed over waterfalls that looked like leaky pipes. I had to fit into his new life because I wasn't sure what my own new life was going to look like.

We did things we never did at home, like visiting art galleries, going to shows and sporting events, and plenty of people came to visit. John would be off during the day and for a period I enjoyed being a domestic goddess, shopping at the markets for dinner and getting back in shape, but eventually the novelty of being a tourist in a new city started to wear off.

OUT OF THE BLUE ONE afternoon I got a Facebook message from one of the boys in the US. It contained a horrific video and Josh said, 'Take a look at this — is it real?' It was the live footage of the 2019 mosque shooting in Christchurch. When I first started watching it I couldn't believe what I was seeing. Immediately I shut it down and rang New Zealand.

A friend confirmed it was real and I just went into shock. I messaged all the boys and told them not to watch the video because it *was* real. They didn't believe me.

I knew I would know people who attended that mosque, and I also knew this event would tear out the heart of every Muslim in New Zealand. As race relations commissioner I was keenly aware of the racist hatred and abuse that Muslims faced every day in our country. Every time ISIS or another terrorist group carried out an atrocity overseas, Muslims living peacefully in Aotearoa became the victims of more abuse. The Muslim community, and especially the women, were constantly concerned for their and their children's safety. Some of those women became close friends and I know how hard they fought to get the government to take their concerns seriously.

In my opinion, if the police and other intelligence agencies had monitored white extremists as closely as they monitored suspected Muslim terrorists, no one would be saying that those murders came as a surprise. The sad irony is that many of the victims had survived ISIS, followed by long treks to safety and months of subsistence living in refugee camps, only to die at the hands of a white supremacist in New Zealand.

Hatred is alive and well in New Zealand, and on that day it walked around the streets of Christchurch with an automatic weapon.

A new race relations commissioner still hadn't been appointed, eight months after I had vacated the role. Part of me wished I was still there, and part of me was relieved I wasn't. I found out very quickly that a woman I knew had lost her son that day. My heart broke for her. The only comfort is that as Muslims they believe those loved ones go on to eternal paradise.

I WAS ALREADY GETTING ITCHY feet, but this tragedy made me even more keen to get home.

I have spent most of life looking for the next thing, and I realised now how lucky I had been to have worked at and experienced things that had real meaning and purpose. Someone once told me they were envious because they had never really been passionate about anything. My problem is the opposite: I get too passionate. I pour my heart and soul into everything, and I eventually discovered there can be a cost attached to that MO.

The truth is, I have kept reinventing myself. I never wanted to be defined as just or only a sporting champion. From a young age my pursuit had been to be the best in the world, and I got there. But what next? When I stepped down and started a family, I never really considered what the next 30 years might look like.

Now I am grateful for all the curve balls I encountered: they opened up whole new worlds. Yes, there were challenging times, but I feel I have made the most of the opportunities and experiences that have come my way. Not to mention my greatest achievement: raising four gorgeous young men.

When I was approached in 2019 about running for mayor of Tauranga, I was honoured — and intrigued. This time I was far more aware of the implications of taking on a major public role. But I knew the issues facing the city, and I understood something of the relationship between central and local government. The more I thought about it, the more determined I became to have a crack.

I discussed it with John — who said he knew I had already made up my mind — so we set the wheels in motion. First up was to establish a strong campaign team, and then we would announce my candidacy. Alex had just graduated and flown to Melbourne, and we were about to embark on a family trip to Josh's graduation in the US. I planned to announce my intentions, then enjoy this holiday, knowing that when I got back it would be full steam ahead.

College graduations are a big deal in the US and we always took the opportunity to get the gang together for a family holiday. Things happen a little differently there and you don't get the final notice that you are graduating until a week or so before. Obviously you know whether it's on the cards, but if you are not on the top rungs it can be quite a nervous wait for those final results. I remember walking around downtown Manhattan when we got the great news that Josh had graduated.

It really was something to celebrate, given that Josh had been hobbling around in a moon boot during this holiday. A couple of months prior to his final exams he had been to Nashville with a group of college buddies for spring break (as they call it in the US). We'd received one of those ominous phone calls telling us not to panic but . . . Josh was in hospital with a broken foot. That's what you get when you do a back flip off the stage at a concert in Nashville. After having major surgery to stabilise his foot with rods and screws, and weeks with a cast, Josh was lucky with the timing in the end and had the cast removed a few days before the holiday.

It was quite a sight watching him cross that stage in the moon boot. I glanced at John and his face showed the same mixture of emotions as mine: relief and pride. There has never been a dull moment raising Josh. He pushed all our buttons, but along with all the challenges he has provided us with lots of laughs, lots of love and some precious memories — and his graduation was certainly one of those.

After the formalities we enjoyed another classic family holiday, heading to Nashville, Memphis and New Orleans. John and the boys are all music buffs so this was the perfect trip for them. The highlight for me was seeing the squash court at Graceland. Who knew Elvis played squash?

Meanwhile, I began to question my decision to stand for mayor of Tauranga. Rather than feeling excited by a new challenge, I was anxious. Perhaps it was too soon after my experience at the Human Rights Commission, and I would be jumping out of the frying pan into the fire. John would still be in Melbourne and the boys were scattered around the globe.

Was this role what I really wanted? And more importantly, was I ready?

Once again I consulted my friend and confidante Paula. She had spent her life in local government, having been CEO of the council and then a long-serving regional councillor.

After lengthy consultation and discussion, and a lot of reflection, I decided to withdraw from the race. I felt I was letting a lot of people down but I knew it was the right choice. In hindsight, given the shit-show that unravelled over the next few years in Tauranga's local government, I think I dodged a bullet. The council pretty much imploded and as of early 2024 we still have government-appointed commissioners running the city.

Sometimes things are meant to be, or not meant to be.

THE ONE CONSTANT IN OUR life seemed to be change. John was on the move again in his job and we were relocating back to New Zealand. The timing was a bit unfortunate — second son Alex had just decided to move to Melbourne! He was only there a matter of weeks before we left.

Once again, our kids were scattered all over the world and we were in New Zealand, settled like a normal husband and wife. But with the mayoral dream gone, what was I going to do now?

I was becoming accustomed to reinventing myself, but this time was a little different. The boys were well on their way to being self-supporting. The bank of mum and dad was now only the bank of dad, and we were even beginning to think there might be a return on our investment. I didn't know what I wanted to do but I knew what I *didn't* want to do, and that was work full time in a big stressful role that often took me away from home.

By chance I hooked up with a group called Street Kai, ably led by a couple of staunch women who saw the need to support Tauranga's homeless. It was a simple, practical approach to a burgeoning problem. Every Monday night — rain, hail or shine — they set up shop in the carpark across the road from the TCC buildings. I think the choice of venue was deliberate, so that councillors and staff could look out their windows and be reminded of how they had abdicated their responsibilities.

Pip and Tracey would set up trestle tables and coffee and tea stands, and volunteers would arrive with a big meal they had cooked. There was never any shortage of patronage. We knew that not everyone was actually homeless but there was never any question that these people were hungry.

Pip would distribute a few basic necessities from the boot of her car — toiletries, socks and undies. There was huge diversity among the volunteers — everyone had a different story. That's the thing about charity, in a perfect world we wouldn't need it, but while we do, it fills a gap. I volunteered for a couple of years until Covid put paid to the weekly meet-ups.

Pip and Tracey continued to support those who really needed it, and they still do. Women like Pip and Tracey — and Jackie Clark and her team at The Aunties — simply exemplify humanity in action. I love helping people and I'm always the first to put my hand up, but I don't do it *every day*. These women are constants in the lives of the people they help, and that is not charity — it's aroha.

Nine
Covid and
Kiwifruit

NO ONE COULD have predicted what was about to unfold when in late 2019 we began to read stories about a novel virus identified in the Chinese city of Wuhan. Attempts to contain it there failed, allowing it to spread to other areas of Asia and later worldwide.

At the start I, like many others, didn't appreciate the seriousness. It was unprecedented in my lifetime and besides, we were living at the bottom of the world so it wouldn't affect us, surely? It wasn't until the first New Zealand case was reported at the end of February 2020 — and, believe it or not, I knew that person — that we all knew Covid-19 was for real.

On 23 March 2020 New Zealand went to alert level 3, with 48 hours to prepare for level 4 — lockdown.

I remember waking up on the first morning of level 3. We

live on a bustling main road in Mt Maunganui, and there was not a car in sight. It was eerie. The weather was glorious for late summer, and we were encouraged to go for walks locally, but it was odd watching people — generally in ones or twos and the odd family group — all giving one another a wide berth as if everyone was the enemy. Everyone was working out how to remain socially distant on narrow footpaths.

You would recognise someone you knew and then realise that having a chat at close range was no longer acceptable. It was as if we had suddenly woken up from the apocalypse and this was our new life.

Just a few weeks earlier we had tramped in Akaroa with our walking group, and a week ago we had watched our son Julian get silver to Nick Willis at the New Zealand Track and Field Championships in Christchurch, but all of that seemed like a lifetime ago. Now we were all tuning in to 1 p.m. daily media briefings from the prime minister and the director-general of health. Joining the team of five million.

We were all thrown into a new unknown. There were stories of panic buying and fears we would run out of toilet paper or flour. We were coming to terms with the detail of what we could and couldn't do but the overarching message was that this was all necessary because New Zealand was 'going hard and going early', to stop this virus from making serious inroads.

It was surreal. I naively thought, *Well, this will all be over in a couple of weeks and the world will get back to normal.* Now we understand that those were unprecedented times.

The novelty for me wore off quickly. I am most definitely not a stay-at-home person and because I wasn't working at the time,

I struggled to fill my days. It didn't help having the attention span of a gnat.

I looked forward to my daily trip to the supermarket — not that I needed to go daily, but it was an outing. I also got into a routine of running around the nearby Bay cricket oval. Two and a quarter laps around is roughly 1 kilometre.

So that was my daily routine, pretty harmless I thought, until one day there was a knock at the door and a young policewoman asked to speak to the owner of a black Mini parked on the road. That would be me.

Apparently there had been a complaint that I was breaking the rules as I had been seen leaving too many times during the day. *Geez*, I thought, *people must really be short of things to do.* I explained to the police officer that the supermarket was a daily run, and that Blake Park was within the 1 kilometre allowed. Her wry smile indicated that she was only following up to placate the aggrieved party.

I didn't know who had complained but I had my suspicions and would always politely wave or toot my horn if anyone was around when I got in my car.

I did, however, break the rules one day. We had been contemplating for some time getting another dog, and received an email from a breeder saying they had a puppy suddenly available. The lockdown meant it wasn't able to go to its planned new home so were we interested? The attached photo cemented the deal. The only problem was that the puppy was in Rotorua, obviously way out of the travel jurisdiction.

I got up in the early hours one morning and drove in the pitch black to pick up the newest member of our family. I had rehearsed some story of puppy rescue in case I got stopped by the police.

Little Frankie, a gorgeous border terrier, was named after an old school friend of John's — so old in fact that John hasn't seen him for over 50 years. So, Frankie Stickleman, if you are out there, you have a namesake!

Frankie and Josh, who was living with us after getting stuck in New Zealand by lockdown, provided hours of entertainment, which was welcome because I was going around the twist, the complete opposite to John, who was relishing not having to travel and enjoying countless hours walking the beach.

AT LEAST I WAS GETTING fit and my daily ritual of laps around Blake Park became more and more laps. But at home I was going stir crazy until I had a lightbulb moment. I kept seeing and hearing advertisements for kiwifruit pickers and packers. Josh and Jamie had both had a crack at that as a holiday job a couple of years prior.

Jamie proclaimed it was the worst job in the world and didn't last very long. Josh agreed that it was the worst job in the world but stuck at it a little longer.

I thought they were soft — how hard could it be? So I decided to apply, my drivers being: 1) I would show them; and 2) I would get an exemption to get out and about and it would fill in the long days.

I responded to an ad on Facebook to pick kiwifruit in an orchard out near Te Puke. When I arrived two things struck me: I was the oldest by a country mile; and, from listening to the various accents around me, I was possibly the only Kiwi.

It was back-breaking work done at breakneck speed. I considered myself fairly fit but found, as those sacks got heavier, that as hard as I tried, I couldn't keep up with most of the younger crew. I did note, however, that not everyone was going hell for leather, and some would slack off until the person in charge appeared marching up and down the vines yelling instructions.

At the end of the day we were told we would receive a text if there was work available the next day. I got a text that night and naively thought I had passed with flying colours, so duly turned up the next day to see some familiar faces.

There was no time for chit-chat — we were straight back at it. Honestly, I was knackered, but I thought I would get used to the manual labour. It took me a while to work out that we got paid by the bin, so the more bins we filled, the more we got paid. Luckily, I wasn't in it for the money. I wasn't filling as many bins as some, and got the odd stare as if to say, 'What the hell are you doing here, old lady?'

Even more exhausted after the second day, I drove home and waited for the text. I waited and waited and nothing. That silence continued for a few days until I messaged the contact I had been given, to ask what the story was. Still nothing, so I sent a text. 'Am I too old, too slow or too ugly? Either way can you let me know if I am needed.'

'No' came the response. 'Okay,' I said, 'just pay me for the couple of days — you have my bank details.' Silence and more silence. Like I said, I wasn't concerned about the money but there was a principle here. I didn't know who exactly I'd been texting but early one morning I found someone who looked like they were in charge.

They were left in no doubt that I needed to be paid. The other pickers, mostly foreigners, looked on confused as I ranted on about human rights and fair pay for fair work. Eventually the money came through. It was a pittance but that wasn't the point.

Undeterred by this experience, I applied through a recruitment agency for a packing job. Surely I could do that, especially when local growers were getting desperate for people to do the work.

On my first day at the coolstore we were taken through a health and safety briefing. It was a short video about mask wearing, hand washing and so on. Then, with no instruction on what to do, we were directed to different stations in the packhouse. I stood by a conveyor belt and watched those kiwifruit come barrelling towards me.

I had worked out that the general idea was to get them into a box or a tray, but they were coming much faster than I could handle and kiwifruit were spilling out everywhere. You could spot the first-timers a mile away, so I wasn't the only one looking like a complete dork.

The clip-boarders, as I called them — I later learnt they were floor managers — were not at all sympathetic. They simply looked annoyed at having to deal with such incompetence.

But there was this one amazing woman who would just appear out of nowhere to help those of us who were in complete disarray. There would be kiwifruit falling everywhere and silently she would swoop in to help clean up the mess and surreptitiously demonstrate the A to Z of packing kiwifruit.

Once I had instruction from the master, I was off and there was no stopping me.

I got chatting to this woman. She had previously worked at our coolstore but now had another job. She had been called back to help out because they were so short-staffed. Her main job was a night shift for another food distributor, so she was working a full day at the packhouse and then going to work. I was in awe of her. This was not easy work — there were people who turned up for one day and were never seen again.

As we were walking to the carpark one day after our shift I saw her kids coming to pick her up. I said, 'Your mother is amazing. I hope you look after her,' to which they replied, 'We do — she is our queen!'

The work was tough mainly because it was so relentless. There weren't many roles around the joint that gave you any opportunity to slack off. Everything was managed like clockwork. Fifteen minutes for morning tea, which meant that by the time you had been to the toilet, washed your hands and got your cup of tea, time was nearly up. The whirring conveyor belts weren't waiting for anyone.

I gathered that the staff weren't the usual packhouse team; before Covid they had relied heavily on seasonal migrant workers. Everyone had a different reason for being there. Some had lost their jobs through Covid, some were young foreign visitors on their big overseas adventures who got stuck here because of lockdown, and there were even retirees looking for extra cash.

Word eventually went around that Dame Susan was in the packhouse and people were curious to know my story. One day while I was packing my boxes — and, I might add, I had become quite proficient — the manager of the coolstore came up and introduced himself. I sensed they may have had concerns that I was masquerading as some undercover investigator. He looked at me rather incredulously when I explained why I was there. I don't know whether he believed me.

The work was tough but I got used to it. I could handle the physical side but the menial aspect was a tad more difficult. In fact 'monotonous' is an understatement for performing the same simple task hour after hour after hour. I had a brief stint at a different station, sorting through the fruit to pick out the ones that wouldn't make the export grade. That was even more tedious, and the time went even more slowly, so I went back to packing.

But there are good people wherever you go in life and I met some great people, all with interesting stories.

I lasted the season and in fact I became a bit of a poster girl. At the end I was approached by the New Zealand kiwifruit association to see if I would be available for a couple of interviews. The angle was locals getting in behind the industry to save the day. The reality of the job for me was an excuse to get out of the house, and I was using my pay packet to buy myself the newest Dyson vacuum cleaner.

EVENTUALLY LOCKDOWN LOOSENED AND THINGS began to open up again. Sports clubs had been seriously affected so there was great relief when the squash club reopened, and I started giving a few lessons again.

Around this time the tom-toms were beating about the state of New Zealand's squash administration. It wasn't just your usual disgruntled punters, it was coming from all directions — parents, players, coaches. Something was not working and people were tearing their hair out wondering what to do.

A lot of them were wearing a path to my door. Often I feel like people see me as Mrs Fix-It, but the truth is that people come to me because they are frustrated trying to get something done and they know I am not afraid to ask the tough questions. If I can sort out a problem I will. So I began to collate all their concerns, and pretty soon could see a pattern to the grumbles. There were serious issues with management and governance.

I am well aware that my strengths are my weaknesses and vice versa. I always tackle things with great gusto, often biting off more than I can chew.

I began with a measured and considered approach, posing a few questions and hoping for a positive response. Naturally people don't like being challenged, especially when they believe they are doing a good job. So the hoped-for positive response was not forthcoming and my challenges opened up a can of worms.

It dawned on me fairly quickly that although I had been the patron of Squash New Zealand for many years, it's a figurehead position with no responsibility, and no power. But I had poked the bear and when the chairperson resigned, I felt I had no option but to stand down as patron and put my name forward for the board. You can't sit on the sidelines constantly complaining if you're not prepared to put up.

Governance really isn't my thing anymore — endless meetings where you have to be conscious of your governance role and not getting into the weeds (you can't tell the CEO how you think things should be done). I know myself well by now and I know I can't help letting my frustration show at times. I much prefer a hands-on practical role.

My main reason for standing for the board of Squash New Zealand was to help save a squash facility in Wellington called Club Kelburn. The Wellington City Council was not going to renew the lease because it was so run down, so the powers that be decided to close it. Keeping it going was apparently too hard.

This got up my nose because Club Kelburn was an institution. There had to be a different solution.

Club Kelburn had opened as the John Reid Squash Centre in the 1960s by the former cricketing great John Reid. He sold the club to Squash New Zealand in the seventies and the next 30 years were boom years for squash. There weren't many commercial centres in New Zealand and especially not in such a prime location, a hair's breadth from the Wellington CBD.

As trends changed, some of the courts were converted to gym spaces, which were also hugely popular. Club Kelburn was a great little business that returned a healthy profit to Squash New Zealand for many years. What national sporting body wouldn't give their right arm to have such an asset?

Part of the success was down to the manager, Rob Walker, who had been there for 25 years. The problem was that Squash New Zealand hadn't invested appropriately in the upkeep of the building and it now needed serious (and expensive) remediation.

That's when I met Gary Murdoch, a longstanding member of

the club with a total commitment to saving it. He rang me for support and that was the start of our campaign.

A board member now, I challenged the board's decision to close the club and we got a reprieve of three months to develop a rescue plan. Club K is what the project was called.

Gary sent out a call to action and clearly wasn't going to take no for an answer. I reckon if he hadn't got his way he would have padlocked himself to the entrance and a bulldozer could not have removed him.

I know some members of the board were quietly hoping I would fail. At one point one remarked that if the trading account wasn't the same in three months, I would personally have to pay the whole lot back. I like nothing better than a challenge — and throw in a good scrap and I am in my element. I didn't know anything about running a commercial squash club, but I did know about galvanising troops. It was a Goliath challenge, but it's always amazing to see the power of people who are committed to a cause.

My motto for service, especially in the not-for-profit sector, is that if you put your hand up to be on a board, then you go, give or get off. If you decide you want to be part of it, you roll up your sleeves and get in there, or make way for someone else who will. Volunteer organisations, including sports clubs, generally have limited human and financial capital so it's critical that everyone adds value.

My first visit to Wellington was for a working bee to remove and/or paint over all the graffiti that adorned the building. All sorts of people came out of the woodwork; they were passionate about the club remaining — or couldn't say no to Gary!

But unfortunately it wasn't as simple as a lick of paint. The place leaked like a sieve and needed a new roof, there was asbestos to remove and a whole heap of other work to bring the building up to standard. None of this was cheap and, to its credit, Squash New Zealand eventually came to the party with $300,000 of the approximately $500,000 we needed. But we still needed more money to fill the gap.

I was overwhelmed by the amount of volunteer support. We kicked off the project with a big launch to which I invited Minister of Sport Grant Robertson to play a game of squash. It certainly helped that Grant was also the deputy prime minister, the local member of Parliament and an all-round good sort.

I was quite relieved to have another project on the go. I managed to get an exemption to travel during Covid and made the long drive down to Wellington more than a few times. Air travel was expensive and limited. But then Covid threw another spanner in the works and the gym and squash centre were closed again.

Between lockdowns and other challenges we completed the major upgrades and the place started to hum again. I was finding it difficult to oversee things remotely, even with frequent visits, so I decided to move to Wellington for a period.

I had mentioned to John what I was considering, and then I woke up one morning and was off. He rang me during the day to ask what was for dinner and I said, 'I don't know, I'm in Bulls.'

'When are you coming back?'

'I don't know that either.'

As it turned out, I wasn't back for six months.

I rented a little studio flat in Newtown, not that I was ever there. I worked my bollocks off — I was at the club twelve hours a day, seven days a week, for nearly three months.

I immersed myself in the project: there is so much satisfaction in turning around something that was destined for the rubbish heap, and knowing you made a difference.

I am slowly beginning to extricate myself with fewer and fewer visits, but to be honest I have developed attachments that are hard to break. Each time I go back I catch up with all the regulars, and there is something unique about the culture of Club K. As much as it is a gym and squash facility, it is also a little community that took on Goliath and won. The place looks amazing — she is an old building and we all continue to give her the love and attention she deserves.

One of the things I have learnt in life is that nobody is irreplaceable, and it is as much of a skill to know when to leave as it is to stay. But there will always be a place in my heart for Club Kelburn.

So, what to do next? Before I had too much time to ponder, I received the phone call that led to my debut on reality television.

Ten
Celebrity
Treasure Island

OUT OF THE blue I got a message to say Chris Haden was trying to contact me. Chris is the son of the famous All Black Andy Haden, and he had taken over his dad's sports management business, Sporting Contacts.

I wondered why he wanted to talk to me, and decided he probably wanted someone's contact details. It never in a million years occurred to me that he would be wanting *me* for something. My days of gigs were well and truly over. So I rang him as I was sitting in my car after a gentle jog on a hot summer's day at Mt Maunganui.

We chatted a bit: Andy had sadly passed away the year before. Andy was such a good guy and he had put together some great deals for me over the years. I wouldn't have made him rich, unlike his star client Rachel Hunter, but he was the man back in the day. I thought it was fantastic Chris had taken over — the last time I had seen him he was a teenager.

Eventually he got around to the matter at hand: would I like to appear on *Celebrity Treasure Island*? I burst out laughing. Surely my use-by date for such things was well past. I was 58 years old, for goodness' sake! It seemed absurd.

I had seen snippets of the show, and my interest was always piqued when people I knew or around my age were contestants, like Barbara Kendall and Sir Buck Shelford, but I certainly wasn't an avid fan.

My first question was about the physical requirements, bearing in mind that my heart at the time was still racing from a gentle jog around the Mount. Cunningly, Chris sold it as no big deal — I suppose that's what agents do! My major concern was all the water contests. The name *Treasure Island* conjures up visions of a *lot* of water and I have a deep-seated fear, especially of deep water. The minute I can't touch the bottom I panic, and this is exacerbated in the sea.

Equal to my fear of water is an absolute dread of wearing a swimsuit — in fact I don't even own one. Ask anyone who knows me well and they will say I'm definitely not vain, but over the years I have become more and more self-conscious.

I also know from experience that me getting a leg and bikini wax leaves the beautician exhausted. I became so mortifyingly embarrassed I gave up going. I did not mention this to Chris . . .

So, with those phobias in mind, was this the best show for me?

Chris said he was sure I'd be able to swim 25 metres in open water, which was the most I'd have to do. He made it sound like a walk in the park (of course). So I began to wonder whether this might be an opportunity to have another crack at overcoming my long-term aquaphobia.

Chris said I didn't have long to decide, which made me think I was the last cab off the rank and they must've been getting desperate. I told him I would think about it, have a chat to John and let him know.

Everyone at home laughed when I told them. But they also seemed excited and keen. I didn't exactly share their enthusiasm but, with their encouragement, I thought, *What the hell.* A tropical island holiday with a bunch of strangers didn't sound too bad . . . I rang Chris back and said yes.

We watched some of the previous shows, and the more I watched, the more concerned I became. I convinced myself my appearance on the show would be just a cameo. Fingers crossed I would not be the first voted off, but after that I could depart gracefully.

My first mission was to purchase a pair of togs — nothing glamorous but something that would do the job. Tentatively I began with a few laps at Baywave, the local pool, trying to find a time when no one else would be around. Eventually it dawned on me that swimming in the local pool where I could always grab the rope in the middle was not a particularly rigorous training environment so I took John, and Julian's partner Lauren, to the harbour side of the main Mt Maunganui beach.

Pilot Bay is generally calm and the two of them stood 25 metres apart as I flapped my way between them. It felt like swimming lessons for babies — minus the floaties. I powered on. I couldn't do chin-ups anymore, and I was a bit slower on my feet, but I realised there was still plenty of stamina in the old girl yet.

The weeks flew by and D-Day arrived, in February 2022. I was met at Kaitāia airport and dropped off at a small two-bedroom Airbnb in the middle of nowhere. I have spent quite a lot of time over the years in Northland so I had a pretty good idea of the surrounds. I was a couple of kilometres from Houhora and also from Pukenui, where the nearest shops were. My main concern was where I was going to satisfy my coffee fix . . .

The other twenty cast members were in a motel in Kaitāia, getting to know one another and doing publicity shots. At the last minute the producers had decided that I would be kept separate and brought onto the show a few days in, as a disruptor or intruder. I can't recall how it was worded but I just went with the flow.

Covid was still around and everyone was taking extreme precautions, so my meals were dropped off at the door. I was told I had to hang out there for a day or so until I got the call-up.

Tragically I got a message the following day with the shocking news that rugby star Inga Tuigamala, one of the show's participants, had taken ill on the Friday night he arrived and been airlifted to Auckland Hospital. Inconceivably, Inga passed away on the Sunday, with his family at his side.

I was devastated. I knew Inga — everyone did — and I immediately assumed filming would be postponed. Separated as I was from the rest of the cast, I could only imagine how awful it must have been for them. They had spent the day with Inga, and several of them, like Ron Cribb, Melodie Robinson and

Mike King, knew him well. It must have been so traumatic.

I was soon told the show was going ahead. It sounds a bit corny to say it's what Inga would have wanted but it probably was. Information was coming my way in dribs and drabs and I was getting a bit frustrated. There was an online group chat but given I was a surprise guest I wasn't included.

After spending the weekend alone I was itching to get started. Despite instructions not to leave my digs I had made a daily trip incognito to the local shops to get my morning coffee and in the afternoon wandered down to the local bay. I was tempted to do a bit of swimming practice but was still so paranoid about the water I was scared stiff I might get into trouble and wouldn't get rescued. Better not to venture in alone, I decided.

In the morning I was up early and raring to go when I got a call to say that one of the cast had Covid. So that meant at least another five days in isolation. Then another cast member would get it. It was like a superspreader event, which was hardly surprising.

I was beginning to have second thoughts about the whole thing. But the weather was still warm and I was in a lovely spot. I couldn't really complain. I discovered that the owners of the Airbnb had moved into their garage to rent out their home to the TV crew. The owners and I could see each other and waved politely. They were an older couple, so I suppose it was a good opportunity for them to make a bit of money.

One day there was a knock at my door and the owner said, 'We know who you are and why you are here, but your secret is safe with us.' Despite knowing we were supposed to keep our distance it was nice to have a bit of company, and a couple of evenings we snuck behind the garage for happy hour with some locals. *Celebrity Treasure Island* was in its second year in this location and was a mini-boost for the local community, many of whom had rented out their homes. They welcomed us with open arms.

IT WAS TEN LONG DAYS and a lot of Covid tests before I got the nod that the other contestants had started, and I was heading out the next day. Just as well — I was nearly tearing my hair out, but I felt for the crew, who I knew were juggling multiple challenges. Looking back, and knowing more now about Covid, I realise it was a miracle we got started at all.

The show had a resident psychologist. The previous year she had been at the end of a phone but this season she was staying nearby — in fact she took my spot in the Airbnb, and when contestants were 'eliminated' they spent the night with her before being shipped off back home.

Steph was a cool woman and nearer my age than anyone else I had met so far. We had already chatted on the phone and I was curious to know whether contestants reached out to her and for what. She had worked on the set of *Married at First Sight*, a real trainwreck of a show, so by comparison I thought *Treasure Island* was probably a doddle. Such is human nature that I found out she was often in high demand for a pep talk or as someone to offload to.

We'd been waiting so long, my presence was by now probably the worst-kept secret in Northland. The rest of the cast had already spent a day/night on the so-called island. The first show had determined the teams and captains, and I was to make my grand entrance at the end of the second day. I wasn't nervous but was slightly apprehensive. I hadn't done anything before in my life that could prepare me for this. My bags had been searched for any contraband and I was such a newbie and a goody two-shoes I hadn't worked out how to conceal any treats. I would know for next time . . .

The first thing that struck me when I saw them all was how young they were. Barring a few, I felt like a dinosaur. I was wracked with embarrassment as I walked out on set at the end of one of their challenges. I can still see the look of shock on some faces. Others had no idea who I was. What the hell had I signed myself up for? Oh well, there was no turning back now.

I was supposed to be a surprise but my reckoning was that people had figured it out. All these people had been holed up together for over ten days and relationships had started to form, so I didn't only feel like a disruptor but a complete outsider. The extra twist was that I was made a team captain, which saw someone else demoted and went down like a cup of cold sick. It was such a terrible start which did *not* help my popularity.

I decided someone must have spun a few yarns about me because there was obviously a preconceived idea of who and what I was. It was odd, meeting most of these people for the first time, to know that it wasn't my reputation that preceded me — half of them hadn't been born when I retired! If part of the game strategy was to pit people against you from the start, it was working well.

Celebrity Treasure Island could best be described as a weird social experiment. You throw a bunch of strangers together, half starve them, deprive them of sleep and all creature comforts, and stand back and watch what happens. It's a recipe for some interesting interactions, to say the least.

I had had plenty of time to do my homework while in lockdown. It could possibly drive you around the bend watching repeat episodes of *Celebrity Treasure Island* end on end, but I wanted to find out everything I could about what the challenges were like, and see whether I thought I was capable of doing this stuff without making a complete fool of myself.

My age had never worried me till now. I had always prided myself on staying fit and active but one day it just creeps up on you — that moment when you know there are some things you will never do again. The mind is willing but the body really isn't, and it's frustrating as hell.

I pretty much felt like an outcast from the beginning but it didn't perturb me unduly, as I had no intention of staying around long.

I got a bit of a shock at first about the living arrangements. I had genuinely thought that what the audiences saw was purely for television, and that the actual living conditions would be a little more luxurious. Nobody would really be expected to survive on burnt beans and rice.

Got that wrong. What you saw was what we got. It was basic and as rough as guts. I was so lucky I was used to roughing it. My beauty regime wasn't too fatally interrupted, but my eyes were on stalks most days when I saw half the women arrive on set with a full face of make-up.

It's the producers who determine how you will be portrayed on the show, and part of me was self-conscious about that, but after my first few nights I gave up worrying. My greatest downfall was forgetting I had a microphone around my neck and a lot of ears were listening to my every word. Also, something you said one day might be played in a different episode — these were the sorts of surprises I got once the show went to air. I found it looked like I didn't give a hoot, but I did, until actually I didn't.

What I knew would test me was lack of sleep and coffee. If I don't get enough of either, things can get ugly. So I was stuffed both ends of the day.

The first night was like being on school camp. When the sun went down there wasn't much to do, so everyone turned in early. There were two groups of women: the mature women in one hut and the younger, hip crew in another.

Holidays by the beach are usually quite relaxing, listening to the waves lapping on the shore, but we were only metres from the sea so it was more crashing than lapping — even with earplugs the noise was disconcerting. Sleep for me in normal circumstances is difficult and I attribute it to menopause, along with the hot flushes, the mood swings, the irritability and the brain fog. Good to get all the excuses out up front. The first few hours of each night I sleep, then I wake at regular intervals until I just can't lie there any longer.

I wasn't sure how I would cope here if I was sleep-deprived; it wasn't as if I could excuse myself every day and go for a nana nap. There weren't too many there who could empathise either — I was old enough to be just about everybody's mother.

At least here I had the stars to gaze at, until we were hit by electrical storms and lashing rain. That was about when the resident possum family took a liking to our pad.

It was disconcerting — we had no watches, no phones, nothing to read or to occupy the time, and not even the ability to make a cup of tea (let alone coffee). So by the time the sun came up and my fellow campers started stirring I had been up for hours. A few days more of this and I'd be a raving lunatic.

I desperately wanted to go home, but as captain I had immunity from elimination and no one could tell me when that was going to finish.

THE DAYS WERE FULL ON. The camera and sound crews arrived early, always hoping to catch a little cameo of the morning rituals. Then the story producers turned up. I worked out early on that they were the ones running the show. Each team was assigned a team of story producers. They hold a lot of information about what's coming next but they play their cards close to their chests. Masters at manipulation is how I would describe the story producers. They had to manage all the twists and turns of the game and, more importantly, the personalities playing it.

They must have dealt with a lot of unhappy contestants struggling with a whole raft of issues. The story producers saved the day for me, offering encouragement by lying through their teeth and telling me it got easier; stroking my ego by saying I was doing really well ('for someone my age' they didn't actually say but it was what I knew they were thinking).

The strange thing is that although there are around twenty of you, you have barely any interaction. Sure, you spend time together during the challenges, but otherwise they keep you apart. The crew yell out 'ICE!', which means no chatting to one another. So if people weren't chatting, how on earth were they managing to form alliances and make deals? I was so naive.

Take the women's alliance, for instance. Last time I checked, I identified as a woman, but I was never invited to be part of the main women's alliance and neither were some others. It was obviously an Exclusive Women's Alliance.

I definitely wanted to win some money for my charity, The Aunties, but I never really thought about strategy. Initially the thought of winning was far from my mind. My best bet, I decided, was to try to win some of the charity challenges. They were less demanding and had an element of luck and the opportunity to cheat just a little, so they became my focus.

When we weren't filming challenges we spent a lot of time regurgitating our day in one-on-one interviews to camera. Often they would get behind in filming these, so on day five they would ask me something about day three and I had no idea. I hated that part but some of the cast loved it. They would be away for hours talking and acting out how this and that panned out.

There were a lot of personalities, and some who genuinely believed their lives would be changed by starring in *Celebrity Treasure Island*. So there were people who were themselves, and others pretending to be someone else.

The days just rolled into one another. Every morning I would wake up and think, *This is unbearable, someone please get me out of here*, and then at the end of the day I would think, *This isn't so bad. Perhaps I can handle another day.*

Elvis Lopeti summed it up: 'This is a silly, silly game.' The whole charade *was* a silly game and it came with silly rules that I paid absolutely no attention to.

Rule number one: Do not leave the perimeter of your campsite. There was too much action and no free time during the day to do that anyway, but given my night-time wakefulness I did take to wandering around during the night. There were security guards dotted around the place but they were generally asleep in their cars. After all, it wasn't Alcatraz — what on earth were a few so-called celebrities going to do?

But I kept my explorations clandestine from the crew. When, on the odd occasion, a security guard did notice something, I would lie commando style on the ground. They would do a quick whip-around with the torch and then go back to sleep. Easy, and I would be on my merry way.

During our travels in the day I had noticed little cabins dotted around the farm and quite a big setup which I found out was the art department. There were some little treasures in there — finding a jar of coffee was a eureka moment for me, as were any other little treats I could escape with. The key was to only take a little so it wouldn't be noticed.

I only had a couple of scary moments. Once a dog chased me. I was petrified, but mainly it was shock at encountering it in the dark. Then on an excursion to the furthest camp I got a bit disorientated in the pitch black and walked straight into an electric fence. I screamed more out of fright than anything else.

It became a ritual. More than anything it was something to do and something to talk about. When the rest of the team woke up in the morning they were always interested to hear about the Dame's nocturnal escapades. They quite enjoyed the treats, too, especially a bit further down the track when I noticed that the art department had had a barbecue and there were a few beers and some RTDs left in the chilly bin. We felt like kids who had got stuck into their parents' liquor cabinet.

The coup, though, was after Karen O'Leary was eliminated. The morning after each elimination they got brought back on set to do their post-show interview. We didn't see them but we knew they were around. We had arranged that Karen would buy some wine and beer at the local store and hide it in the Portaloo. She is a top sort, and boy, we enjoyed that wee drop shared between us. It was even worth all the trouble we got into.

Eventually I got sprung — I had taken a packet of Tim Tams won in a challenge by the other camp. I thought it was quite an achievement in the middle of the night, especially as it involved a steep climb. One of the episodes shows me getting a warning from Matt the host, and being threatened with expulsion. I kept doing it, knowing it was probably an idle threat and actually I couldn't have cared less if I was sent home.

I dreaded the water challenges, not simply because of my fear of open water — I was equally aware of not wanting to embarrass myself or be a liability to my team. It turned out I wasn't the only one terrified of the water, but I managed not to baulk or refuse to participate, despite sometimes wanting to.

We were seriously tested at times. I am tough and don't mind roughing it but I draw the line when there are serious health and safety concerns. I imagined the crew all tucked up in bed in their warm accommodation at night, never fully understanding how horrendous it was for us a few times when we really had to battle the elements. One night a bad storm blew through the camp and the combination of wild wind and torrential rain kept everyone awake all night. I was genuinely frightened that some of the wooden beams were going to break and cause serious harm.

The boys erected tarpaulins to keep out some of the rain but it proved futile. In the end we all sat huddled together, miserable and wet. I thought, *They can't possibly leave us out like this all night,* but no one came to our rescue. This called for an evacuation and I knew there was a little bach up the hill where we could seek shelter. The security guards looked somewhat perplexed when we all arrived with our sleeping bags. The small house had mattresses; it was warm and dry and blissful. It reminded me of being on a marae.

Luckily, we didn't spot the rat until the morning. Possums I can handle but if I had seen that rat crawl over Siobhan's sleeping body I would have run for the hills. I think that was the first time everyone was seriously thinking, *What the hell are we doing here?* We were over it.

In the morning we were admonished for leaving the campsite and I thought, *You have got to be kidding me — it's just a television show!* As if that wasn't bad enough, in the aftermath of a severe storm we were made to do a water challenge. I just lost it — I sat down on the sand refusing to budge. But in the end, despite feeling totally exhausted, somehow I did it.

Grit and determination are in my DNA. Despite being older and slower, I was not giving up. The harder the challenge, the more determined I became. Things I could have done easily 20 or 30 years ago were now so much more difficult, but the mind is a powerful tool and pain is only temporary, so I never (well, hardly ever) threw in the towel.

I was hanging on by a thread and seemed to have taken on the role of mother hen. When Melodie left I became cook and cleaner as well. Uber didn't deliver to our island, so someone had to cook the rice and beans.

All around me people were stitching up deals left, right and centre and I was oblivious. I was sneaking out to meet others but mainly to share food. No doubt I was also trying to catch up on the gossip, but it was great to let off steam with kindred spirits — or at least I thought they were.

There were good and bad days — every day had an element of both. What would start as a cracker could end up a catastrophe.

Our team got pretty good at winning challenges but there was one that drove me to breaking point. It was an individual challenge — every person for themselves. Again, winning was never my goal, which was purely and simply to try to look competent and not come last. And not be humiliated.

We had to dig a hole under a large log that was embedded in the sand. The digging wasn't the tough part, it was finding the courage to crawl under. Each time I tried I had visions of being stuck with my head in the sand, unable to breathe. I am very claustrophobic. Finally I gave up and sat like a sad-sack on the log.

Then I noticed that the only others left were the really big fellas, who were going to need longer to dig a hole big enough. Someone had found a way to disadvantage some of the big, strong guys and kindly offered me a chance to get through, but it was too late by then. That was possibly the worst moment for me in any of the challenges: the combination of anxiety and unadulterated humiliation meant I was in a foul mood for the rest of the day.

The rest of my team had made the next round and I spent hours on the windy beach waiting and waiting. They all finally turned up, full of the joys of spring, which did nothing to help my mood. We then proceeded to watch the challenge's big finale to see who would take out the ultimate prize. It was obviously not me so I didn't really give a shit, but I should have paid more attention because that was when Jesse Tuke, who I must say was looking very strong at this point, won the golden ticket. What we didn't know at the time was that Jesse's prize was being taken to see where the treasure was buried. That defining moment gave him a massive advantage over the rest of us.

On the beach that day I did everything in my power to control myself but I was so angry. I felt like I had been abandoned and no one gave a toss.

The most anxious time of every day was pre-elimination, when you knew this could be your final day on the show. I felt such contradictory emotions, in one breath begging to go off but also secretly hoping I would survive another day. I was realistic enough to fall on my sword a number of times by volunteering to be put up for elimination but was turned down, which was embarrassing because in effect it meant I wasn't viewed as much of a threat. And I had my uses — cooking, cleaning, stealing and finding out information.

I nicked a pack of cards once, and even the odd newspaper I found in one of my favourite haunts. The cards were a godsend, and hours and hours of Presidents and Arseholes filled in some long evenings.

The crew eventually gave up worrying about the contraband, so long as everything was out of shot when they were filming. When the numbers dwindled to just one team the rules were relaxed even more. The odd coffee with powdered milk was good for morale.

But there were still days when people got quite down. The weather had turned and most days were miserable. Clothes were damp and filthy and all people could think about was a nice hot shower.

I got a surprise one day when the producer said my husband John had emailed her. We were three weeks into the show — well, probably four, given the delay at the start. It was probably the longest time in our 40 years together that John and I hadn't been in contact. We had vaguely thought that I may be on set for a few days and then suddenly reappear back home.

She said he asked if I was okay and said the family missed me. She had replied that I was fine — up to all sorts of mischief but still there and still alive. I was quite chuffed, but I have to confess I hadn't really given him much thought. Being cut off from all contact and technology had been hard at first but became quite liberating after a while. We would occasionally beg the crew for news from the outside world, only to be told Russia had just invaded Ukraine, Australian cricketer Shane Warne had died and Covid was still rampant.

We travelled with the crew to various sites for the different challenges and wore masks when we did, and we had the odd Covid test. But thankfully (and somewhat miraculously) there was no more Covid on set.

AFTER THE SHOW FINISHED FILMING it took me a while to adjust back to normal life. I had never envisaged getting to the final six so had not expected be there for over three weeks — in fact a month if you take into account the early delays with Covid.

I had just wanted to put up a good showing, even if it was only for a few days, and win some money for The Aunties, a charity helping vulnerable women and children who have experienced domestic violence. Chief Aunty Jackie Clark (not to be confused with Jackie Clarke the singer) is someone for whom I have enormous respect and admiration.

I am a great believer that women are the lynchpins of families — if Mum is okay then the children will be too. The Aunties have a passionate commitment to supporting women who leave violent relationships, and their children. It is vitally important work and I would have loved to win more for them.

We had told people I was going on a yoga-cum-health retreat, away from civilisation, but after a few weeks of texts, calls and emails going unanswered people began to get suspicious. Those who were really concerned or needed something that couldn't wait contacted John. He allayed some concerns, and let the cat out of the bag to a few trusted friends. I gather that there were mixed reactions. Some had assumed I was on *Dancing with the Stars*!

It would be hard not to learn something about yourself from an experience like that. At my age there wasn't much about myself I didn't already know, good and bad. But there were a few lessons. Although I had got a little obsessed about my age and my ageing body I discovered there was life in the old girl yet. And while it's been commented on a lot during my lifetime,

I even acknowledged to myself that I am gutsy and determined and I never give up. There had been plenty of opportunities to bail but I had hung in there till the bitter end.

It wasn't easy keeping mum — there is a long wait between filming and the show going to air. I was starting to forget it had even happened when I was notified it was imminent, and the pre-publicity started to ramp up.

Seeing myself in television advertisements and my face plastered on a bus shelter made me cringe. I started thinking back to that really difficult time and wondering how they were going to portray me. That part is completely out of your control so I became quite nervous.

With the odd exception I didn't watch any of the episodes live. Not knowing how I was going to come across, I didn't feel comfortable sitting watching it with others.

After each show I would get comments while walking the dog or at the supermarket checkout, and the odd text. Young children would say, 'Hey, there's that old lady from *Celebrity Treasure Island*.' So then I would sneakily watch the episode on demand. My memory had faded a little and I was embarrassed by some of the silly things I did — like playing Big Booty Big Booty. Some of the comments that came out of my mouth left me gobsmacked.

Still, it wasn't all bad. Among other things, I found a whole new fan base who were completely unaware that I had actually once upon a time been a world squash champion.

The Spinoff ran a weekly roundup of the show. I thought they summed me up pretty accurately by saying that if there was anyone whose persona was completely different to what you thought, it was Dame Susan (or Dame Suzy, as I became known). They added that if you asked her friends and family they would probably tell you that's exactly what she's like!

I have a big personality and I think that came through, but so did the fact that I am soft as marshmallow. I can live with that.

WHEN IT WAS ALL OVER I could relax. *Never again* was my one thought. That was my one and only crack at reality television. But then Chris Haden came calling with another proposal, this time with a twist.

I had mentioned to one of the producers that I thought my son Josh would love this sort of thing. Chris wanted to know whether Josh might be interested in doing a series with me in a new format, *Fans v Faves*. Yes, I have three other sons, but I thought this would be the last thing they would want to do alongside their mother. Josh, the ultimate prankster and risk-taker, is not easily embarrassed!

This show was only two weeks, the format was different and the destination was Fiji — at least we would be warm. Josh would love it. I had no grand illusions of winning but I thought it wasn't impossible, and it would be a few extra dollars for my charity.

I had experience under my belt and some unfinished business, I decided. There is a lot of luck involved, and perhaps Lady Luck would look on me kindly.

The changed format brought back previous contestants (Faves) and pitched them against Fans (including Josh). It wasn't until I arrived at Auckland Airport that I discovered who my fellow contestants were. The Fans had already left and were kept apart from us until we got to the island.

It was quite a different vibe being seasoned pros; there was this overwhelming sense of déjà vu — good and bad. Having done it before certainly gave us an advantage. Four girls, four guys; some already knew each other or had been on the same shows. The only person I had met before was Alex King. Aside from Josh Kronfeld, I felt like the oldie of the group, but it was good to be in with the others from the start, and not separated out on my lonesome.

Making television programmes is demanding work for all involved. The days are long. Even the first day was a marathon — consumed with publicity shots, interviews with media. We had to get dressed up and made up. All that palaver with hair and make-up is not my favourite pastime but I just wore and did what I was told. Putting up a fuss just meant things took longer. I have always believed that people are just doing their job, and if you can make it easier for them you should. The saying 'Hurry up and wait' is just so true. There are so many nuances to filming a scene it can be a real test of everyone's patience.

We arrived quite late in Nadi and had to make the long bus trip to Suva. If you have travelled in Fiji you will understand this journey takes time; the road conditions stretch a two-hour trip to four hours, especially travelling at night.

Halfway through the journey we had a pit stop. It was well into the early hours of the morning by now. I patiently waited on the bus for ages while people were nattering outside. Then I suspect I confirmed my reputation when I yelled at the top of my voice for everybody to get back on the bloody bus so we could get to our destination. I saw some strange glances, as if to say, 'She really is as scary as I was told.'

Cast and crew stayed at the same resort before the show and it all felt much more relaxing this time around. Or perhaps I was just an old pro. I was anxious to know how Josh was getting on. Word had got out that my son was on the show. I know who spilled the beans and it wasn't me.

The weather was atrocious. Forget blue skies and beating sun — there was the odd good day but mostly it rained and rained and rained and everything was muddy and boggy.

Josh was in boots and all, as I knew he would be. The toughest part for him would be after filming — keeping it all under wraps until the series went to air.

Once the news leaked that Josh was my son the crew decided to have him disclose it in the opening episode. We all were introduced, and after the formalities hosts Bree and Jayden asked if anyone from the opposing teams knew one another. There were some odd looks when Josh calmly said, 'Gidday, Mum.'

Insomnia was once again going to be my biggest challenge and it didn't take long before I began my usual night-time excursions. Locals had been employed as security guards and at the entrance to the compound was a sentry-type office, large enough for one person.

Our first encounter took them by surprise and took some explaining. There were three Fijian locals, two men and a woman, who were all asleep in and around the sentry box when I turned up. I explained that I was a contestant, to which they nodded furiously. 'Yes,' one said, 'you are the old lady on the show.' They meant no disrespect — that was how I became known. It got so that when they started their shift every night at midnight, they always asked the changeover crew if the old lady was still in, meaning had I been eliminated.

I would while away hours chatting to them over a cup of tea. They were so grateful to have the job, as it paid more than their usual occupations on the island. Well, it really wasn't an island but we were all pretending it was. On nights when it was raining cats and dogs we would take shelter in the art department, a series of farm buildings being used to house the props and materials for the challenges. Once again, I had my eye on the odd packets of biscuits, the coffee and a few other treats I spotted.

Some nights I would arrive and they would be fast asleep on the concrete floor. I couldn't understand how they managed it but was told you can do anything after a session on the kava. I heard about their lives and their families and we struck up quite a friendship — until we got sprung. After that, the art department was locked at night and we were back to the sentry box for our soirees. I had some serious explaining to do to the producers so they wouldn't lose their jobs.

I discovered that they thought that if I won the $50,000 it was mine to keep. Clearly they believed they might be in for a share, so I explained that it was all for charity, and that there wasn't much chance of me winning anyway. We made a pact: I promised I would repay their kindness for keeping me company during those long evenings. And sure enough, the day after the final they turned up at the hotel for their bonus. It wasn't much for me but was probably a week's wages for them.

I snuck out twice to see Josh at the other camp. I didn't have any nefarious intent but others didn't see it that way and I was castigated by my own team. It was a fair cop, but I didn't really care. He had a target on his back, partly because he was my son, but also because it was obvious from the outset that he was physically capable and therefore a threat. When the teammates he had formed an alliance with were eliminated he became enemy number one probably for both teams. It was quite likely they all wanted to get rid of both of us.

Josh and I had of course agreed that we would each do whatever we could to support or help the other, but this proved easier said than done. In my first show a person had fairly and squarely been eliminated but someone else had stood up and sacrificed themselves instead. This was certainly something I would have done for Josh but the producers, sensing ahead of time that I would probably do anything to keep Josh on the show, had made sure it couldn't happen by adding a specific clause to my contract.

Josh got eliminated but didn't go down without a fight. I was really disappointed to see him go — in fact the very next night, when I was put up for elimination, I nearly threw in the towel. Part of the attraction this time around had been sharing the experience with my son.

On the other hand, it did mean I now only had myself to worry about.

I suffered all sorts of minor injuries. My skin is like tissue paper — another sad reality of getting older — so I was always nicking something that bled profusely and inevitably got infected. The medic made daily visits, checking everyone's movements (particularly the bowel ones), and picked up that my leg was badly infected.

The local doctor prescribed some antibiotics. I doubled the dose, to speed the healing, and became severely ill. I suspect taking them on an empty stomach was part of the problem and I vomited violently. I was already running on empty and actually became a little delirious. People told me later I was madly running around the hut telling people to give me back my phone. I was taken off site to where the medics were staying. Oh, the joy of a proper bed, and dare I say it I sneaked a shower. The next day I woke feeling like a new person.

I was asked whether I wanted to continue on the show and I said I would if I could get some decent food. The reply was a simple no, so it was back to beans and rice. It was worth a try.

On the Fiji show every night seemed to conclude with a game of Would You Rather. As in: Would you rather shave your legs with a cheese grater or poke a pin in your eye? I didn't really get into the spirit of the game but just sat and listened quietly.

Perhaps the tropics had got to people but the questions became more absurd, more gruesome and more ridiculous as time went on. Probably because I was old enough to be just about everybody's mother, I did feel a little awkward and even embarrassed because I didn't always know who or what they were talking about.

One night I couldn't resist slipping into the game with: 'Would you rather sleep with Lance Savali or Art Green?' (Both were contestants.) That got everyone's attention. So the Dame was listening after all. No one answered.

Unlikely friendships were formed during these silly social

experiments and that, for me, was the ultimate prize and surprise of the whole experience. What you don't see on screen is what happens when there are no cameras around, and the interesting conversations that come about within this unlikely grouping of people. Never in my wildest dreams, at this stage of my life, had I expected to form such special bonds.

Eleven
Seeing
the World

I HAVEN'T SEEN all the world but probably more of it than many, and I haven't finished yet. There is still time to visit new places, revisit some old favourites and tick off a few bucket-list adventures.

I acknowledge that not everyone has enjoyed the opportunities I have, but I can unashamedly say they have come from a lifetime of hard work — and a bit of luck. As they say, you create your own luck. I was fifteen when I got on an aeroplane for the first time and travelled to the Gold Coast to represent New Zealand at the Australian Junior Squash Championships. I can vividly remember the excitement, which was twofold: I had never been out of the country before, and this was my first time wearing the silver fern.

In fact I was lucky to get there. Mum drove me up to Auckland in my brother's prized Holden Torana, which was a little more powerful than the Hillman Avenger she was accustomed to driving. Too powerful, as it turned out — she failed to stop in time at a red light in Remuera, wiped out a set of traffic lights and wrote off my brother's car.

Luckily we were unhurt, but Mum was in shock. (Apparently she was right as rain after a few stiff gins.) Meanwhile, our team manager, Susie Simcock, came to the rescue and offered to drive me the rest of the way. The last thing I recall my mother saying to her was, 'Susie, look after Susan, and if she comes back gay, I will hold you responsible.'

Mum wasn't homophobic, although her comment obviously was. She had somehow picked up this irrational belief that every sportswoman was gay and therefore I was probably destined to be as well. It was that generation — I'm sure if she was alive today she'd be mortified at that statement.

I also learnt a valuable lesson on that trip about telling the truth at all times because you *will* be found out. This is a message I relayed time and time again to my sons.

We were staying in one of those high-rise apartment buildings in the heart of Surfers Paradise. Towards the end of our trip we were asked to clean the vehicles we had rented for our stay. I am not sure what possessed me — perhaps I was trying to show off — but I decided to take the car I was cleaning for a spin around the block. All was going well until I came to park. I misjudged the brakes and smashed the car into the parking barrier.

I begged my teammates not to blow the whistle. I wasn't sure how I thought I was going to get away with it, but I had visions of my entire squash career being over if people found out.

We were called to a meeting and the powers that be asked what had happened to the car. To their credit, everyone denied all knowledge. Then Neven Barbour, the men's manager, asked me directly if I knew anything, to which I said no. He said, 'That's strange — we saw you driving.' My face reddened and I burst into tears. It turned out that twenty storeys up they were watching the whole drama unfold.

WE NEVER WENT ON FAMILY holidays growing up. Almost the only travelling I remember was to sports events, mainly squash tournaments. We visited relatives around the country but we never went camping or to the beach. My good friends had a caravan at Papamoa and I begged Mum to drive me over for a couple of days. I can't remember why but she flatly refused. I was in my early teens but already pig-headed so I walked there — it took me all day and half the night.

Man, I was in a power of trouble. The look on my mother's face when she drove to pick me up was truly frightening and I was grounded for eternity.

We certainly never went to any sunny Pacific islands or theme parks, but neither did any of my friends. I really wanted to, and nagged and nagged my parents to take us on a summer holiday. Finally they succumbed and took my brother Gerard and me on a trip to the South Island. I was twelve and he was seventeen, and not exactly enamoured with the thought of spending three weeks with his baby sister and his parents.

Mum and Dad had booked a caravan at Tāhunanui Beach in Nelson. The plan was to drive down from Rotorua, catch the ferry across the Cook Strait, spend a few days at the holiday park and then tow the caravan down the West Coast.

This was new territory for my folks but they quickly got into the caravanning life. Not much to do all day but catch the rays and chat with the neighbours. Mum and Dad loved to chat, and they especially liked happy hour, when all the holidaymakers would bring out a few beers and sit chatting until the sun went down.

Gerard found other teenagers to hang out with, and I was just delighted to be on holiday with my mum and dad. Everyone was happy and contented. In fact the time flew by and we never left the campground — that was the sum total of our South Island holiday.

BACK THEN I COULDN'T HAVE predicted that my life would come to involve so much international travel. When I left Rotorua in 1982 bound for the United Kingdom, aged eighteen, I was so naive. I thought catching a flight from New Zealand to Heathrow would be like catching the bus from Rotorua to Auckland. As a mother now, I wonder what on earth my parents thought about their only daughter embarking on this massive adventure. I had chucked in my last year of school, so if it all failed I had nothing to fall back on. What on earth was *I* thinking — a young woman trying to make it in a minority sport with no plan B?

After a tough couple of years eventually I got established. By this time John was on the scene and we had a pretty nice life based in the UK for about ten years. It sounds glamorous now and it probably was, but I was busy and didn't concern myself too much with my surroundings. I didn't fully appreciate it until later.

Travelling from competition to competition didn't allow much time for sightseeing. I travelled extensively through Europe but I would arrive for the tournament, compete, then leave after the final for the next competition. I was so fixated on training I wouldn't have dreamed of taking a day off to see the sights, and I believe this was part of the key to my success. I never woke up in the morning overwhelmed with the success of winning the day before: it was always on to the next one, and what do I have to do today to be better than I was yesterday. This was the cycle for many years, so it didn't really matter where in the world I was.

The circuit back then was Europe for the first half of the year, then down under for the rest. Then there was a smattering of tournaments in Asia and North America, where squash was becoming more popular. The other attraction was the sunshine circuit in South Africa. They offered big money — more than we had seen in our careers — but this was in the apartheid era, so in effect it was a bribe. I didn't ever go. I was criticised when I started at the Human Rights Commission for having even considered playing in South Africa, but in my playing days I was naive to the intersection of politics and sport. The reason I didn't go was that an anti-apartheid activist group threatened to blow up my parents' house.

My parents had never travelled overseas so I was delighted to be able to shout them their first overseas trip to Europe in

1986. Dad was born in Dublin but spent his first birthday on the ship when his parents immigrated to New Zealand. It was a thrill for them to visit the country of his birth, and more of a thrill for me to have them in the crowd to witness me winning a British Open.

Our tiny council flat in Marlow was overflowing — some of our flatmates moved out for the duration so my folks could stay, and we even had Peter Bidwell, a New Zealand sports journalist, crash on the couch. We would listen to him tapping away on his typewriter in order to get the story away the next day. Who today could imagine having the journo stay at your house during the most important event of your career!

We met a guy in the UK who was some sort of life coach, who said something that resonated with John and me. He told us to always celebrate the achievement, big or small, so we decided that at the end of each European season and after the British Open we would take a week's holiday to recharge the batteries and reflect and plan.

It was magical advice, and we had some fabulous trips — to Eilat in Israel, the Canary Islands, and many trips to Honolulu because that was the Air New Zealand stopover on our way back home.

One night I'll never forget was during our visit to Eilat. John and I used to play cards a lot, especially Five Hundred. I must have been a sucker for punishment because he always won but I relentlessly kept on trying. One night after a few drinks we started playing again and we made a bet. The person who lost had to stand on their head stark naked and drink a glass of beer.

By a sheer miracle — or perhaps because of all the beer John had drunk — I won. John duly fulfilled the bet — shame we didn't have mobile phones back then to provide the proof. Thirty years on, in 2022, we were in the Grand Canyon and attempted to re-create that scenario. This time I lost, but because of the advent of mobile phones there was no way I was going to follow through.

JOHN'S FAVOURITE SAYING IS 'ADVENTURE is the champagne of life'. I am not as adventurous as him, but over my lifetime I have given most things a crack when presented with the opportunity. There are limitations, of course — I could never see myself jumping out of an aeroplane, and I have definitely become more cautious as I have aged.

Two things scare me: water (as mentioned earlier) and flying. My fear of flying has never stopped me travelling, but I don't enjoy it and always get extremely anxious.

Overcoming my fear of deep water has been more challenging but I have tried over the years, long before I agreed to do *Celebrity Treasure Island*. In 2005 the founders of the New Zealand Ocean Swim Series, Scott and Natasha Rice, reached out to me to see if I would be keen on participating in one of their first events.

The very thought sent shivers down my spine.

Scott hadn't known about my aversion to water. I could bob around a hotel swimming pool but I was petrified of the ocean. It wasn't a concern about what lurked under the surface, it was the fact that if I couldn't touch the bottom I panicked and would be overcome by a fear of drowning.

Years ago, aged thirteen, I was caught in a rip at Little Waihī beach and if it hadn't been for a good Samaritan rescuing me I would have drowned. I have lived with that fear all my adult life.

Scott suggested I take some swimming lessons, and I really thought working up to conquering an ocean swim would be a good opportunity to overcome a phobia. It would certainly be up there on the scale of massive personal achievements so I thought I would give this a real crack.

I began swimming lessons at the polytech pool in Tauranga. It was used for water polo and diving instruction, so the deep end was deep. I was comfortable only as long as I could hang on to the side. But each lesson saw incremental improvement and slowly it got a little easier and my confidence grew.

I was quite chuffed with my progress, and then one day the swimming teacher said, 'I hope you don't mind me saying so, but you have a rather unusual mole on your back.' I am covered with moles and freckles so this one must have really stood out.

I made an appointment with a skin specialist and had the mole removed. As I had a few stitches down my back I had to stay out of the water for a while. The specialist rang a few days later and said, 'You should buy a lotto ticket. It was a melanoma.' I needed some more moles removed, but he said I was one lucky person.

Unfortunately — sorry, Scott! — that signalled the end of my swimming career. By the time the wounds had healed I had lost the enthusiasm and never did that ocean swim . . .

BY THE WEIRDEST COINCIDENCE, AT the same time my friend Jenni also had a melanoma removed. It got us talking about our mortality, and one thing led to another, and pretty soon we'd decided to take an overseas trip together with our kids to celebrate our good luck. We had recently sold our house in Auckland so had money in the bank. It was not exactly earmarked for a world tour but we thought, *What the hell.*

Organising four months' travel for eleven people was a massive undertaking. Luckily Jenni was a whizz online. She enjoyed organising and admin, and she had an eye for a bargain. Airbnb didn't exist in those days but there were similar websites, and we were travelling in the off season, so it was all doable. The dream came to life, and we left New Zealand in September 2007 for the trip of a lifetime.

Some time ago our house was burgled and my laptop was stolen, with all our photos, so I have had to dig deep to remember this adventure without the pictures to bring back the memories. All up there were seven children, ranging from eight years to fifteen. Despite it being so long ago, the kids all have very fond memories of that holiday and it's been fascinating to hear what they remember and what has stuck.

John couldn't take the whole four months off work so I set off with our boys and Rochelle, who had looked after the boys in the past. She would help me with them until John arrived, then go off on her own adventures. She was well aware of what a handful they could be at times, so I was grateful for her support — and boy did I need it at times.

Each family stayed in their own accommodation but always in close proximity. We also had our own vehicle. It stood to reason that a family of all boys and a family of all girls would have different interests and sometimes want to do their own thing. But it was cool watching the relationships between the kids develop, and to this day those girls are like the sisters our boys never had.

The main idea of the trip was to spend a few days in a big city, being tourists and seeing all the main attractions, then head off for a week or so to a local village or town. We thought travelling in the off season would be cooler, less crowded and less expensive. It didn't always play out that way.

We knocked off Hong Kong, London, Rome, Barcelona and Paris, interspersed with varied and sometimes rather interesting stays in smaller places. Looking back, the highlights were sometimes the simplest things — like playing kick the bucket in a small, deserted French village called Saint-Thierry.

We found we quickly blew the budget going to big attractions — it wasn't cheap taking eleven people to anything, so the weeks in the villages made the money last longer and gave everyone the time to recover from the hustle and bustle.

Gearing a trip around children certainly had its challenges. We would plan to spend all day at the Louvre, and the kids would have rushed through the entire museum while John and I were still at the first exhibit. They didn't ooh and aah at the Colosseum or any Roman historical site — they were more interested in the street hawkers or the con men playing craps and ripping off unsuspecting tourists like their mother.

Of course they loved the theme parks, and interestingly preferred the local ones with the big rides to Euro Disney. In particular we came across Gardaland Park in Italy, near the small village of Colà. I think they would have easily gone there every day. In fact one day we adults left them there with Rochelle and hurtled 200 kilometres down the motorway to have lunch in Milan. They were none the wiser when we returned.

Boy did we thrash our rental cars, even if packing and unpacking at every new destination became a chore.

We travelled to Austria to a place called Zell am See, where it was magical being in the mountains. John and I are not skiers but the boys wanted to have a go. We met some young skiers on the gondola going up and paid them to take the boys for a couple of hours. They loved every minute.

We did a few things that wouldn't necessarily earn us good parenting awards. Internet cafés were becoming all the rage in Europe and we would pile the kids into one and buy them two hours online. They had strict instructions, and Club Penguin was the only game we let them sign up to.

Their parents would then whisk off to the nearest pub for a couple of drinks and some respite from the young ones. If the locals at the pub were friendly, we would feed the kids and put them in front of the computer to watch endless box series of *One Tree Hill*.

It was a real adventure. One day they'd be skiing down Austrian slopes, then the next we'd drive all the way to Antibes and be swimming in the Mediterranean. I need no photos to jog my memory about the disasters and the things that didn't go to plan. Like the week-long gastro bug in Carmignano, or the 300 euro in cash that flew away because I had forgotten it was on my lap when I got out of the car ...

We had Christmas in Paris, by which stage funds were running really low, then finished off the trip with a couple of cheap weeks in Thailand.

There is no doubt Kiwis are travellers and our boys were so fortunate to have this opportunity so young. Their sporting talents have seen them all score other great overseas trips, and their years at college in the US have meant they have already seen much of the world.

Twelve
'Women's Things'

MY FIRST WORDS to camera when I appeared in *Celebrity Treasure Island* were: 'I'm here to represent menopausal women!'

My mother never talked to me about female health or 'women's things', to use her term. Perhaps it was a hangover from having six sons, but I figure it was also a generational thing. Her mother obviously hadn't talked to her about such things either, because she told me that when she went into labour with her first baby, my oldest brother Brendan, she had no idea what to expect.

She was back in that maternity wing — run by nuns — only eleven months later and said any discussion about sex or even childbirth for that matter was still taboo.

What we kids didn't figure out until years later, when my father passed away, was that Brendan had been born before they were married, hence the black wedding dress (which we were told was because there was a war on). When Dad died we were all saying how sad it was they hadn't reached their fiftieth wedding anniversary and then it dawned on us that Brendan was nearly 51 . . .

In my teenage years Mum didn't warn me about getting my period. I attended a Catholic school where there was no sex education at all. If you were lucky you may have picked up something in biology class, but my entire knowledge was gleaned from other girls' conversations or snippets I picked up eavesdropping on my brothers. I was incredibly naive.

I tried to broach with Mum the subject that I thought it was odd that all my friends were getting their periods but I wasn't. Mum told me I was lucky and shouldn't worry about it. I had no sisters to confide in, so I just let it go.

Eventually, when I reached eighteen and still had not begun to menstruate, I divulged my concerns to our team manager. After that came a barrage of medical tests and I was discovered to have primary amenorrhea. In short, I was a very late developer, which was an actual medical condition. I was told to carry on as normal. Not that I knew what normal was anymore. The only caveat explained to me was that down the track I might struggle to conceive. Well, that certainly wasn't on the horizon and of no concern at that moment.

I finally got a period at 21, and it hit me for six.

I WAS TWELVE YEARS OLD when my mother had a hysterectomy, at St Andrew's, a private hospital in Rotorua not far from where we lived. She was 50. I was simply told she was being treated for 'a woman's problem'. I was assured she would be as right as rain, and she was.

I visited her after her operation and her first instructions were to go home and bring a crate of beer back on my trusty Raleigh 20 bicycle. She stashed it under her bed. The funniest thing about it now is that I didn't even consider it an unusual request. Really? Did I think everybody else's mother had a crate of beer stashed under their hospital bed?

My mother was stoic and staunch; all I recall her saying was that she would have to have a few days off from vacuuming and heavy lifting.

The upside of primary amenorrhea was that I never had the worry of competing while I had my period, and I never used any contraception. So when I unexpectedly got pregnant in 1991, aged 28, it was one hell of a surprise. From then on, all suggestions that I might struggle with fertility were blown out the window — the reality was quite the opposite: I couldn't stop getting pregnant.

After Jamie was born I had a tubal ligation and suddenly it felt like payback time, as if some miserable coot had decided that seeing as I had got off lightly for the past 20-odd years, I would be rewarded with the heaviest menstrual cycles known to woman. I might have been a late starter but now I understood what most women had been going through. I thought it was catastrophic but I discovered it was all pretty normal; I just wasn't accustomed to it.

It's tough being a woman — our bodies go through so much more than men's do, and I felt quite isolated in my life surrounded by males. There was absolutely no understanding or empathy in our household. The only 'discussion' was John driving the boys home and saying, 'I wonder what sort of mood Mum will be in today?' As if it was some sort of game, they would throw their school bags down in the front entrance and wait to see how long it took for me to blow a valve.

I was in my late fifties when my periods stopped — late starter, late finisher. How had I not known that perimenopause can be equally debilitating?

I've only come to realise fairly recently what a major part that whole hormonal rollercoaster played in my behaviour and decision-making over the years. It didn't affect what I did so much as the way I sometimes went about things. My goal was always to be cool, calm and collected but I am a fairly emotional person and sometimes cool and calm went flying out the window thanks to those bloody hormones.

A classic example was a testy meeting among the commissioners at the HRC. It was not my finest hour, even if perhaps it was warranted, but I lost it. I walked out of the office saying, 'This is a fucking terrible place to work!' (I would like to add in my defence that that was the only time I used the f word in the office, although I was sorely tested on many occasions.)

I felt like I was the only one standing up for the staff.

The following morning Jackie Blue, the equal employment opportunities commissioner, asked me for a coffee at the Colonial Cafe on The Terrace. I loved the Colonial; it brought back memories of when my mother would take me out for lunch as a special treat. Good old-fashioned comfort food.

We had a general chit-chat about the previous day's events,

with me assuming we were on the same side. Then Jackie said casually, 'Do you think you are going through menopause?' She went as far as to suggest I get my doctor to prescribe half a Prozac to help with the hot flushes and mood swings.

I am not usually lost for words but that floored me. I assured her my outburst was about much more than menopause — we were dealing with some serious work-related issues.

However, I liked Jackie. She was a doctor who had been a breast surgeon, and I knew she was genuinely concerned about me. What's more, I can now see that she was probably right on the button. My behaviour had been very erratic of late. However serious the work issues were, I know my hormones were not helping the way I was handling it.

Until then I hadn't talked about menopause with any of my friends, let alone perimenopause — what even was that? I remember I would often stay with a friend in Auckland. We would be in the middle of watching a television show when she would get up and go to stand outside in the freezing cold, complaining of feeling hot. I just used to laugh. At that stage I was still having periods.

It suddenly wasn't so funny when it crept up on me. I had no idea what was happening to me — literally no idea. Was I just really tired? And really hot, because it was summer? And why was I so angry — an almost out-of-body feeling of rage, totally out of proportion to the event? What was all that about?

No one I knew seemed to be affected, or they weren't telling. I knew that for some women it's a genuinely low-key event and I guess I assumed that I too would meander through with limited consequences, and it would be done.

Working at the HRC could be stressful, so I just figured it was stress making me angry and insomniac, and turning me into someone who kept forgetting mid-sentence what she was about to say. I had a male doctor but was generally pretty healthy so didn't have to go that often. When I did, nothing was ever mentioned about the dreaded change of life.

John noticed I was a bit tetchy — or more so than normal. It wasn't hard to tell — if he stacked the dishwasher the wrong way, didn't clean the microwave after he had splattered stuff in it, bought the wrong brand at the supermarket, he wore it.

When it started to dawn on me, I sent him a message on one of his overnight trips suggesting he might like to do some homework on the effects of menopause. His deep dive included a glance at Wikipedia, and he returned a snapshot with the words 'irritability' and 'mood swings' circled. His attempt at humour was not appreciated.

So if this was menopause, what was I going to do about it anyway? I knew there was hormone replacement therapy, but like many women of my generation I associated HRT with an increased risk of breast cancer and heart disease. Everyone had been using patches until a big study in 2002 deemed HRT to be a killer. After that report staggering numbers of women went off their HRT immediately and it remained out of favour for many years.

I just kept muddling on, thinking, *Well, I've got this far — I am going to be 60 soon and it's all downhill from there anyway. These symptoms must surely start dissipating soon.* I tried all the natural remedies, all the dietary recommendations that came into my social media feed promising to help, but nothing worked and I was getting desperate. I feared for John's life.

It wasn't just the moods. I would be giving a speech and the words would just disappear from my brain. I lost my keys, forgot to take money from the ATM, lost my credit card on more than one occasion . . .

For me the turning point was watching the Davina McCall documentary *Sex, Myths and the Menopause*, which came out in 2021. I even made John watch it, hoping there might be a lightbulb moment. Watching other women share their stories, I realised I wasn't completely bonkers — it was real.

Eventually I gave in and tried HRT. The effect wasn't immediate, but very quickly I noticed my sleeping improved. I went from waking multiple times in the night and being wired from 4.30 a.m. onwards to only waking once or twice and even making it through to 6 a.m.

I am on an overseas board that has meetings at 5 a.m. New Zealand time and I have never set my alarm because I am always awake, but this one time I didn't wake up till 6 a.m., missing all the calls and messages asking me where I was. One morning I slept in till 7.30 — I think John thought I had died in my sleep.

When I first started HRT I accidentally left the tablets on the table one day. We came home to find a half-empty packet on the ground. Our dog Frankie had managed to punch the foil tabs and consume half a dozen tablets. I rang the vet, who thought it was all rather humorous, and I'm happy to say we didn't notice any side-effects in Frankie.

All things considered, apart from menopause and a melanoma scare, I have been incredibly fortunate with my health.

I had been on HRT for about a month before we left in September 2023 for a two-month holiday overseas. Hand on heart, I can say it has been a game-changer for me. I only wish I had started five years earlier and not muddled through thinking it would eventually get better by itself. My hot flushes are gone, I sleep better, the brain fog has lifted and I don't sweat the small stuff. For that I am truly grateful, and undoubtedly John is too!

Thirteen
Women's
Sport

IT'S ALL RATHER ironic. I grew up with six brothers and went on to have four sons.

Growing up, I wasn't aware of any gender inequality. My mother was the boss of our family and there was no question that I could be or do anything I wanted. It didn't matter in the least that I was a girl.

It wasn't until I left home and went on the professional squash circuit that it dawned on me that being a young female playing an individual minority sport was going to be tough. Thankfully there has been progress since, but even today many young sportswomen face that struggle, especially in individual sports.

Cost is another limiting factor in minority sports. I joked

later in life that I wish my parents had put a tennis racket or a golf club in my hand. I'd be rich.

In the early days of my career I was barely making ends meet. I was couch surfing from tournament to tournament and there were times I wasn't sure if I had the fortitude to stick it out. Initially I wasn't conscious of the discrepancy between men's and women's prize money. I wasn't winning any prize money, so it never crossed my mind. But as I rose through the ranks I realised there was a huge gulf, and it wasn't just monetary.

In my last year on the circuit I played in what was effectively the Welsh Open in Cardiff. The event was called the Leekes Classic and it was held in a glass court they erected at the local convention centre. I was so naive back then that I thought 'Leekes' referred to the vegetable synonymous with Wales, but in fact the tournament was named after Mr Gerald Leeke, the seventeenth most wealthy Welshman on the *Sunday Times* rich list, who was the generous sponsor.

As expected, I made my way to the final. For the life of me I can't remember who I played but I do remember being on court and hearing all these people cheering for me. This was not the norm — more often than not people cheered for the underdog. After the match I found out it was a bunch of sporty Kiwis in the VIP box who had been cheering me on. Grizz Wyllie, Steve McDowall and some other All Blacks were in Cardiff for the premiere of the film *Old Scores*, a movie about a fictional Welsh rugby hero named Bleddyn Morgan, who has his life in New Zealand interrupted by a deathbed confession that leads to a replay of a controversial All Blacks vs Wales rugby test.

News had reached them that I was playing so they came to

support me. Rugby is revered in Wales (much like New Zealand) so these former All Blacks were treated like superstars, sitting in the corporate box sipping champagne. As a mere player I hadn't been invited to the VIP area but suddenly my status was elevated, given that I knew these visitors, so I joined the rowdy Kiwi mob for the men's final.

As we were watching Pakistan champion Jahangir Khan, my male contemporary, Grizz asked me how much my winner's cheque would be. I said, 'A thousand English pounds.' Then I added, 'Jahangir will pocket five thousand quid if he wins.' Even Grizz gulped at the difference.

This was fairly standard at the time. The argument was that the punters came to watch the men — it was male players who attracted the sponsorship because theirs was supposedly a more exciting game. And it wasn't just prize money. Often the women playing in a tournament would be billeted by the hosts while the male players enjoyed hotel accommodation. I arrived at an airport once and, while looking around for a cab, saw Jahangir disappearing in a chauffeur-driven car.

Eventually I became very aware of the inequality and wanted to do something about it. In the beginning I wasn't advocating for equal pay but just a larger slice of the pie. Although we women had our own professional body to advocate on our behalf it was a hard slog. The male professionals naturally didn't want their prize money reduced, so they were not our strongest supporters.

All the female players were in agreement that something had to be done, but felt powerless to speak up. They feared that rocking the boat might see some of the promoters just telling us to stick it. Something was better than nothing, and we could be cut off at the knees if we complained too much. Most of the male players were good guys but there was a hard core of sexist, arrogant jocks who looked down on us, quite convinced their game was superior.

It's true that I couldn't beat Jahangir on the court, but that didn't mean the men's game was better than the women's. As I often used to argue, you don't put a bantamweight boxer into the ring with a heavyweight. Women's sport is women's sport, and men's sport is men's. They should not be directly compared.

Eventually progress began to happen down under. My profile was larger than that of any of the male squash players in New Zealand, with the exception of 1986 when Kiwi Ross Norman produced the upset of the century, beating Jahangir Khan in the men's world championships. The powers that be saw that I was probably deserving of the same prize money as the men's winner, but making the whole event equal would open a can of worms.

They also knew I wouldn't back down without a fight. More than once they tried to reach a compromise by offering me an appearance fee, which wasn't uncommon when the prize pool was low and tournaments wanted to attract top players. I agreed to this initially but then realised that if change was going to happen and benefit all female players, this wasn't enough. I would have to take a stand.

It came to a head in the 1990s. My personal sponsor, Honda, was the main sponsor of the New Zealand Open. I certainly didn't want to compromise my relationship with them, but dammit — I was putting bums on their seats and to my mind I deserved equal prize money. It was the right thing to do.

John, my trusty manager and master negotiator, organised to meet the head honchos to discuss the situation, and the outcome paved the way for equal prize money in New Zealand — well, at least for squash players.

I am proud that New Zealand was the first country in the world to offer equal prize money for its open championship. Not until ten years after I retired did women's squash pay equal prize money worldwide.

THE 1980S AND 90S WERE boom years for squash. I was a big fish in a growing pond and I was lucky to have John to manage my sponsorship deals. Sometimes I didn't even know about them until the deal was done — perhaps that was the plan. John wouldn't enter into anything he knew I'd be uncomfortable with but there was one major sponsorship that was a bone of contention.

I need to remind people that this was a time when tobacco and alcohol sponsorship were the backbone of sports sponsorships. (Alcohol sponsorship still is.) John arrived home one day to say he had stitched a deal with Kiwi Lager, a new brand of DB beer. I've never drunk beer so I wasn't that excited, but every few months a truck would pull up in the driveway and deliver 50 dozen bottles of Kiwi Lager. Soon after, my brothers would arrive to pick up their share.

I had a Kiwi Lager logo on my squash tops, and each time I appeared in the paper or on television brandishing the logo, I would be paid a bonus. It's hard now to believe that this was considered okay. It makes me cringe today, but back then we relied on it.

But times and trends change, and squash fell in popularity. Numbers dropped, sponsorship dried up. I have been delighted in recent years to see squash back in the news — the successes of Joelle King and Paul Coll have put squash back on the map.

Like so many squash devotees I have argued for a long time that squash should be an Olympic sport, so while I was writing this I was thrilled to hear the great news that squash has been included in the Los Angeles Olympics for 2028. As a vice-president of the World Squash Federation I was so gratified — it's been a long time coming.

The news sent shockwaves around the world for all squash players, fans and administrators. Squash will in effect be a demonstration sport in 2028 but if we get it right in Los Angeles we have the opportunity to become a full Olympic sport and enjoy all the benefits of being in the Olympic family.

It would supersede any world championship. Inclusion in the Olympics opens up avenues for increased funding in many countries, including New Zealand, so more players can be supported on a professional path. The lack of funding for non-Olympic sports has concerned me nearly as much as the inequality between male and female sportspeople. But in this regard too things are changing — slowly, but they are changing.

I want to acknowledge here the contribution of Labour Sports Minister Grant Robertson, who oversaw significant investment in women's sport in New Zealand in the years 2017–23. No disrespect to Grant but he never seemed the most likely candidate for sports minister, and yet he made a real impact.

New Zealand hosted the Women's Rugby World Cup 2021 and the Women's Cricket World Cup 2022, and co-hosted the FIFA Women's Football World Cup 2023.

When I was growing up there was very little televised sport. I remember my family huddled around the radio listening to coverage of the All Blacks and the Black Caps. Women didn't even play rugby or cricket — the mere thought that women could play these traditional male sports was absurd, and yet look where we are today.

We have made huge progress, but there is a long way to go.

John and I were invited by Wynton Rufer to attend the Spain vs Sweden semi-final of the women's football. We rushed to grab something to eat before we headed to Eden Park. No longer on the A list, we didn't want to have to queue for chips and a hot dog. We needn't have worried — the hospitality in the FIFA VIP lounge was extraordinary: tables lined with gourmet food and Taittinger champagne flowing like water. It was certainly a who's who. We chuckled at half-time watching the minister of sport scurrying around trying to find somewhere to charge his phone.

It was a great game and we, like everyone else there, got caught up in the excitement. Absolutely we need to celebrate and acknowledge the gains for female athletes, but we also need to understand that it will be a lifetime before we host these major events again, and in the meantime, after all the hype has died down, will we continue to see progress towards the ultimate goal of equal pay?

Sad to say, a large proportion of our society doesn't believe in equal pay for male and female sportspeople. They may even be our fathers, our brothers or our sons — and there are plenty of women who don't believe in equal pay either.

If our goal is to change this mindset, then we need to start having informed discussions. We're not simply talking about prize money or salaries — we're talking about equal treatment throughout: access to quality support services, physio-therapists, parental leave, training facilities, accommodation and travel. All elite athletes should enjoy equal access to these basic essentials.

If you're not provided with the same resources and opportunities, it stands to reason you can't perform at the highest level. Not only do women enjoy fewer professional sporting opportunities than men, but they also face far greater challenges and barriers to perform at their best.

It wasn't so long ago that our national women's cricket and rugby teams travelled in economy class on long-haul flights, before being expected to turn on match-winning performances. I know what that feels like. On one trip I was on the same flight as the All Blacks Sevens team. They turned left at the front of the plane on boarding and I went down the back to my rightful seat. When we transitioned in Los Angeles I was chatting to their coach, Sir Gordon Tietjens. God bless him — he had a word to the Air New Zealand crew and I was upgraded.

The playing field was briefly levelled.

In the 20th century, while male sport was becoming more professional and organised, sportswomen continued to be the poor relations. In some cases women's sport was actually discouraged. Many women over the decades have paved the way for change, and the current rise in female sports gives us the opportunity to continue to address some of the long-held discrimination against female athletes. Not only is it the right thing to do, but it will have flow-on effects in other walks of life.

Sport has the ability to change the lives of women everywhere. Sportspeople are major role models, and by paying and treating them equally we are making a statement that we value women's contributions equally.

Our major sports organisations are big businesses. They may not be giants like FIFA, but they deal in big money. We can't continue to allow them to pay your sister or daughter less for doing exactly the same job. If we do, we are still encouraging a culture where women are valued less than men.

Today we see more women as CEOs of sporting organisations, more women on boards and in leadership positions. It's not uncommon to see and hear women commentating our national sports. It's all positive, but equality on the sports field is coming too slowly in my opinion. History will show it's the right thing to do.

Fourteen
Travelling On

IN MID-2023 WE headed back overseas, with Alex and Josh along for part of the trip, to relive some memories and create some new ones. The first thing we all noticed was that everywhere we went just seemed so much more chaotic. The big cities were overwhelming, with thousands of tourists. Maybe it was a post-Covid thing — when the world opened up again everyone wanted to travel. But John and I were keen to start ticking off some of our bucket list.

After much deliberation, and having received his Gold Card in 2022, John had finally resigned from his job of nearly twenty years. It was a difficult decision — he loved the job, and the team he worked with are part of our family. (In fact I often think I may be at the bottom of the pecking order . . .) It's a scary prospect forgoing the income, too.

John had travelled a lot for his job but he worked from home when he wasn't travelling, and this drove me to distraction at times. While he locked himself away in his office, there was no getting away from the constant ringing phone or the late-night conference calls that are a part of working for an overseas company. Selfishly I used to feel that from Monday to Friday our house was his office, not our home.

It was also hard to have a nana nap when John was on a call next door. He never said anything to me but I know he thinks it's rather odd to sleep during the day (even when you can't sleep at night), so there were a few eye-rolls. John always says sleeping is for the dead! Some days I wanted to turn the music up LOUD or stroll naked into his office while he was in a video conference . . . I can be a cow, but not usually that much.

So when he made the decision to resign I supported him, and now we are busy spending our kids' inheritance. I hope they understand: we have helped set them up for life and now they are on their own.

At the moment there is nothing holding us back, and no grandchildren on the horizon, so we have decided to travel whenever we can. We enjoy physical challenges, in particular hiking and being outdoors, although John is far keener than I am. While we still have good health and are as fit as fiddles, we want to get as much under our belts as we can.

For a long time we had been intrigued — actually slightly obsessed — with doing the Camino de Santiago, so we decided that's where the 2023 trip would end up. Sometimes I feel like I am married to Forrest Gump or a mountain goat — any trip away has to involve a physical challenge. On this trip, aside from a few days, we would be on our feet the whole time and carrying all our gear, so we planned to travel with only 6 kilos of luggage each.

It makes travel and transitioning easy — no waiting for bags — but also makes for severely limited wardrobe choices and I do really feel like a bush pig. Three pairs of undies, three pairs of socks, two pairs of shorts, one pair of trackpants, a couple of t-shirts, a rain jacket, a warm jacket and that's it — along with our toiletries. I think it was all part of John's masterplan to avoid doing any shopping . . .

OUR TRIP BEGAN WITH THE 80-kilometre Jordan Trail to the ancient city of Petra with our good friends John and Lynette. I had never been to Jordan. Before we went on our hike we took a couple of days to visit the old cities of Jerusalem and Bethlehem. Jerusalem was certainly on the bucket list, but who could not be affected by the conflict with the Palestinians.

Having met Holocaust survivors like Inge Woolf I was determined to visit Yad Vashem — The World Holocaust Remembrance Center — but we didn't realise it was Rosh Hashanah, a Jewish holy day, so it was closed, along with just about everything else. Luckily we found a pub open. In general, however, I was overwhelmed and overawed by the Holy City and the trip to Bethlehem. We left a couple of weeks prior to the Hamas attack on Israel. It now all seems so surreal but I'm very grateful we all got out when we did.

Our trek to Petra was ably guided by a wonderful Jordanian woman, a donkey and a Bedouin guide through searing desert. We camped under the stars in less than luxurious conditions that seemed like paradise. The local Bedouins put up our camps and cooked our food, and the whole thing was magical — aside from the howling coyotes and barking dogs throughout the night. It reinforced for me that I no longer felt a need to revisit the capital cities of the world. I much preferred getting off the beaten track and experiencing everyday life with the locals.

After Petra we went to Rome, where the highlight was catching up with Alex and Josh and Alice, Alex's gorgeous partner. They had been travelling too, and we revelled in the stories of their adventures. They had been following the All Blacks, as Kiwis do, as well as going to music festivals, running with the bulls in Pamplona, sunning themselves in Greece, riding camels in Morocco — as you do when you are young.

After a couple of days in Paris John and I trained and bussed to St-Jean-Pied-de-Port to begin the 780-kilometre French Camino. There are a few different Camino routes starting in different countries and all ending at Santiago, but the French is by far the most popular.

To be honest, I wasn't really sure what to expect. We are seasoned walkers, having completed most of the Great Walks in New Zealand, and we are also used to carrying all our gear and staying in huts. This was a much larger undertaking, but I confess I left it to John to do the study and prep. He pays more attention to detail than I do and I'm happy to tag along.

It was not a religious pilgrimage for us and I wasn't looking to 'find myself'. I chatted to various others along the way and realised that people walk the Camino for a whole host of reasons. We struck up a number of friendships along the way.

The first day is gruelling but quite beautiful. Immediately after leaving St-Jean-Pied-de-Port in the early hours of the morning we began climbing, and for the first 8 kilometres I was thinking to myself, *What the hell have I bought into?* The climb crosses the Pyrénées and you finish after a very long day in a small village called Roncesvalles.

The first night set the scene. We arrived at our accommodation, which was basic but comfortable, and sat out in the sun with our newfound friends enjoying a couple of drinks. We were tired but not knackered. It had been a tough day, especially carrying our own packs. And this was day one. The test would be repeating it for another 30 or so days.

John and I are both reasonably fit and fairly gutsy but we weren't really sure what to expect — how hard it was going to be and how we would cope. We also knew that being together 24/7 might be a challenge, but it turned out that after 40 years together we still are the best of friends.

Many people doing the Camino stay each night in albergues, which are best described as communal hostels. For about $20 you get a bed in a room with a whole horde of others. Sometimes there is a communal meal but the cafés and bars along the way also offer amazing 'pilgrims' meals'.

The highlight that first night was our first pilgrims' dinner. For a very good price we got a three-course meal and — unbelievably — a whole bottle of wine each. I was initially gobsmacked, but thankfully the alcohol content of this Spanish wine seemed to be a lot lower than New Zealand wine so I never woke up feeling dusty — like I had had a big night.

So the first couple of weeks felt a bit like a pub crawl. We would walk till the early afternoon because it was so hot later in the day. Then everyone would sit to have a drink, and before you knew it, the people you had been walking and chatting with were all sitting around the table and the drinking would roll into dinner. Then we would fall exhausted into our beds. Our routine became early to bed and early to rise.

After a lifetime of backpacking, staying in DOC huts, we were a bit over the whole communal living thing. We gave it a crack a couple of times, but one shower between 30 people, and the cacophony of noise during the night, especially the snoring, was enough to turn me into a raving lunatic. So, where we could, we stayed in small pensions — similar to a two-star hotel but where you have your own room and bathroom.

Not that that stopped the snoring. John has recently taken up this less than desirable habit. I know he can't help it but it's not ideal being absolutely knackered at the end of the day and trying to sleep next to a freight train. Initially it was a gentle word: 'John, you're snoring', to which there was usually no response. When it gradually got louder there might be a nudge or a full-blown kick. Someone once suggested tape over the mouth downwards from the nostrils, but this only changes the tune from the mouth to the nose . . .

Anyway, before we knew it, the daily hike became our norm. At the beginning John and I always walked together, then gradually it became half the day together, and by the end we were both doing our own thing. We knew all the others by then, and we all just walked to our own rhythm. Our little routine was catching up along the way at the numerous cafés and bars. Whoever arrived first would leave their pack outside to let the other know a food or drink stop was in progress.

Friends back home kept messaging me asking whether I had

found myself and I would laugh it off, but it's weird how without you realising it those hours and hours of being lost in your own thoughts begin to have an effect. It somehow gets a hold on you. At the beginning, to be honest, I found it a bit of a drudge. Some days were torture, especially when the wind and rain battered us from start to finish, leaving me wondering about the point of it all. *Is this it? Are we there yet?*

I am not accustomed to long periods just thinking, and to be honest I hadn't been looking forward to that aspect. But I was amazed at how my mindset changed. As we plodded along I went from feeling very woeful about turning 60 and thinking about all the things I couldn't do anymore, to focusing on how much further I could push myself, and even contemplating what the next challenge could be.

There was no particular lightbulb moment along the trail but I did come to appreciate what a wonderful life I have had, filled with so many amazing opportunities and experiences. My life has been full of so much meaning and purpose. It's been jam-packed and full on.

I am truly grateful.

And I'm absolutely up for whatever is to come.

Acknowledgements

I HAD NEVER contemplated writing my memoir until Tess Nichol from Allen & Unwin approached me. Even then it seemed ridiculous! *Who would want to read about the last thirty years of my life?* was my immediate reaction.

It was the encouragement and support from Tess that got me both started and finished. As with most challenges, there was the sense of self-doubt and the dread of putting it out there, but in the end it was cathartic. When I was struggling, Tess always had some words of wisdom to keep me going.

Many thanks to Rachel Scott for her superb editing skills and advice. Thanks also to Leanne McGregor for her talent in bringing it all together, to designer Kate Barraclough and proofreaders Kate Grimstock and Mike Wagg, and to the whole crew at Allen & Unwin. In the end it was a team effort.

I couldn't cover everything — and I haven't — but this book

tells the story of a life well lived, full of amazing opportunities and experiences. Perhaps taking the time to write it down has made me appreciate that, as well as the wonderful people who have shared it with me.

Special thanks to my friends (you know who you are); to my four amazing sons, who have given me the greatest joy in my life; and to John for his enduring patience. As he says, living with me has been a rollercoaster of a ride, and luckily he likes rollercoasters.

About the Author

SUSAN DEVOY was born in 1964, the only girl in a family of seven children. Growing up in Rotorua, Susan was a talented sportswoman, becoming a four-time world squash champion and New Zealand's greatest squash player. Her fierce drive means her life has seen hardly a dull moment. She lives in the Bay of Plenty with her husband, John. They have four boys.